JOHN CABOT

THE DISCOVERY OF NEWFOUNDLAND

B.D. FARDY

Other Books by Bernard Fardy:

Captain David Buchan in Newfoundland
Harry Cuff Publishing Ltd., 1983

Jerry Potts: Paladin of the Plains
Sunfire Publishing Co. 1984

William Epps Cormack: Newfoundland Pioneer
Creative Publishers, 1985

Under Two Flags
Creative Publishers, 1987

Demasduit: Native Newfoundlander
Creative Publishers, 1988

Leifsburdir: The Vikings in Newfoundland
Harry Cuff Publishing Ltd., 1993

JOHN CABOT

THE DISCOVERY OF NEWFOUNDLAND

B.D. FARDY

Creative Publishers
St. John's, Newfoundland
1994

Appreciation is expressed to *The Canada Council* for publication assistance. The publisher acknowledges the financial contribution of the *Department of Tourism and Culture, Government of Newfoundland and Labrador*, which has helped make this publication possible.

∝ Printed on acid-free paper

Published by
CREATIVE BOOK PUBLISHING
A Division of 10366 Newfoundland Limited
A Robinson-Blackmore Printing & Publishing associated company
P.O. Box 8660, St. John's, Newfoundland A1B 3T7

First printing May 1994
Second Printing April 1996

Printed in Canada by:
ROBINSON-BLACKMORE PRINTING & PUBLISHING

Canadian Cataloguing in Publication Data

Fardy, Bernard D., 1949–

John Cabot

Includes bibliographical references.
ISBN 1-895387-35-3

1. Cabot, John, d. 1498? 2. Cabot, Sebastian, 1476?-1557.
3. Newfoundland — Discovery and exploration. I. Title.
FC301.C32F37 1994   917.1804'1   C94-950111-5
E129.C1F37 1994

For a Pair of "Jacks" ...
... who both know the difference

Contents

Foreword

TWELVE YEARS AGO, I had a telephone call from a person who identified himself as a technician who had done some writing about Captain David Buchan, and wanted to know if he could have an appointment with me to discuss whether his materials were worth publishing.

When I met him, I was as much impressed by his modesty and the nature of his education and employment history as I was later impressed with his ability to present historical information in an interesting style. Bernard Fardy made no pretence of being a historical researcher in an academic sense, but enjoyed reading about historical persons as written about in many secondary sources, and summarizing and speculating about the accumulated material. His book, I believed, would appeal to ordinary readers: it was not intended for professional historians. Since that day in 1982, Bernard Fardy has had seven books published—by three different publishers (one in British Columbia). He is still employed by the federal Department of Forestry and Agriculture as senior cartographic technician.

When my friend, Don Morgan, asked me if I would write the Foreword to a book on John Cabot, my first reaction was "Considering what little is known about Cabot, who could produce a book on him?" The answer was "The same person who could produce a book about Mary March."

What Bernard Fardy did was read all he could find about Cabot and about other explorers and adventurers who had visited North America before and after Cabot. As a cartographer, he paid particular attention to early maps and charts relating to Newfoundland and neighbouring areas. He then drew comparisons, made certain generalizations and in the absence of detailed information, deduced informed speculations on what most likely transpired. The result is a readable and interesting book.

HARRY CUFF
April 1994

Preface

WE FIRST HEARD OF JOHN CABOT, like most Newfoundlanders, from our parents, who like good pre-Con-
federation Newfoundlanders, claimed the 'Englishman'
discovered our beloved island home. When we started
school we began to hear about a fellow named Columbus,
and two dates were bandied about which was quite confusing to the first-grader of six years of age. We were also taught
a short rhyme which would ensure we kept the two "discoveries" and the dates straight:

"In 1492 Columbus sailed the ocean blue ..."

"In 1497 John Cabot discovered — Cape Breton!"

Imagine our disbelief! We hurried home to inform our
parents that they had been wrong all their lives. "No, my
son," we were emphatically told, "John Cabot discovered
Newfoundland! That's just a lot of Canadian drivel them
mainlanders have dragged down here since we allowed 'em
to join up wid us in Confederation." That settled it. Those
mainlanders were wrong.

Then imagine our further dismay a few years later when
we took our first "course" in Newfoundland history from a
book approved by the Newfoundland Department of Education entitled *The Story of Newfoundland and Labrador*. (First
published forty years ago this year; we still have a copy of it
on our book shelf.) This "authorized" history of our island
said that John Cabot did not "discover" Newfoundland at all,

but it was in fact some bunch of Norsemen or Vikings or such!

Now we were certain we were having our heads stuffed with mainland drivel. Our biggest concern was how Uncle Mose and the crowd in Pigeon Inlet were going to take this news. They'd threatened to take all the youngsters out of school down there when they were told that Cabot discovered Cape Breton and not Newfoundland. What kind of ructions would that cause?

So after twenty years or so of investigation we decided to try and sort the thing out, Uncle Mose notwithstanding. We can only hope that the crowd in Pigeon Inlet will not be too feisty with us.

B.D. Fardy
St. John's
January 1994

One

Cabot's Antecedents

J OHN CABOT did not discover Newfoundland. Christopher
Columbus did not discover North America. Both were
Johnny-come-latelys in the discovery of the "New World."
The "New World" had already been discovered and forgot-
ten at least five or six times before the voyage of Cabot in
1497.

Initially, North America was discovered by people
moving eastward across land, not by people moving
westward across an ocean. Northern Asian hunters, following hoofed food sources, crossed into North America via the
Bering land bridge as long as 35,000 years ago. They did not
know they were discovering a "new world" and at the time
of their migration across the Bering land bridge they were
not. They were simply following food sources on a contiguous land mass that eventually became isolated by the
melting of glaciers and the creation of the Bering Sea. This in
turn made the Americas waterbound continents and
"created" the New World.

In a natural progression these early "explorers" continued to move southward and eastward until they eventually dispersed throughout the entirety of the Americas. Ever

nomadic, these hunters and gatherers continued to migrate north and east into the area we know as Labrador.

From Labrador, these wandering people, perhaps pressured by more warlike tribes from the south or simply moving from a depleted food source area, saw the hulking landmass visible a mere nine or ten miles distant across the narrow Strait of Belle Isle. About 4000 years ago some of these venturesome Amerindians decided to investigate the "little land" to the east.

Archaeologists have identified these people as the Maritime Archaic Tradition, a culture which flourished and survived in northeastern North America for almost 5000 years. It was they who "discovered" Newfoundland about 4000 years ago.

The migration of the "Red Paint People," as they have been named, from Labrador to the island of Newfoundland was probably slow and not without a considerable amount of danger, given the treachery of the Strait of Belle Isle with its strong currents and savage winds. The culture of the Red Paint People persisted in Newfoundland for over a thousand years until about 1200 B.C. when it suddenly disappeared from existence. The "new-found-land" became lost.

It was "discovered" again about 800 years later, this time from the north by a culture anthropologists have identified as the Dorset Eskimo. The Dorsets are believed to have migrated to Newfoundland from the northern climes of Greenland and Baffin Island following seal herds and fish stocks which were retreating southward in the advance of a mini ice-age which occurred around this time.

Evidence of their occupation of the island has been well documented and they inhabited much of the northeastern coastal areas until about 750 A.D. when they inexplicably disappeared from the island.

After the demise or retreat of the Dorset culture the island was again left to the crash of breakers and the call of gulls. It was not long, however, before the island was "discovered" again. This time it is not certain if it was discovered from without or within.

The people next recorded as "discovering" and inhabiting Newfoundland were the Beothuck Indians, but it is not clear if they "re-discovered" the island from Labrador or were a re-emergence of the Maritime Archaic Tradition. In any event they survived, and thrived on the island for almost 1000 years until they were officially declared extinct in 1829.

The next "discoveries" took place, conversely, not overland from the west but overseas from the east. The first of these is shrouded in the mists of mythology, but should not be completely discarded as being fraught with the fogs of foolishness. Before the Viking voyages there were tales circulating among the Norsemen of an Irish monk who had sailed to the westward from Ireland, Iceland, Greenland and beyond, three hundred years before the venturesome Norsemen sailed westward. Both Ireland and England claim him as a patron.

He is known to history as St. Brendan, and his seven year voyage to the new world with his small band of zealous monks, intent on spreading their fervent mantle of Christianity over the heathen heads of infidels in unknown lands, has been discussed, debated, and debunked by scholars for a century. Yet most myths and legends have a basis in fact.

St. Brendan was born in the late fifth century near Tralee, County Kerry, Ireland. From all accounts he lived a

According to legend St. Brendan and his courageous crew of Irish monks sailed to the new world and explored it for seven years prior to 600 A.D.

very pious and successful life, recruiting enough followers to establish four monasteries in the British Isles as he travelled throughout them for more than fifty years. When he was seventy years old the son of a fellow abbot told him about a "Promised Land of the Saints" far to the west of Ireland.

Even at three score and ten, Brendan was as zealous as ever. Gathering eighteen of his brethren he set out on a voyage of "discovery" to the "Promised Land of the Saints." They set sail in an Irish "curragh," a small, sturdy and very seaworthy vessel which is believed to be the forerunner of the "knarrs" in which the Vikings later made their journeys of exploration. Ribbed and sided with wood, the "curragh" was covered with tanned ox hides instead of planking. Seams were caulked with ox tallow and the tiny ship was propelled by a squaresail. Capable of carrying twenty men, the "curragh" was fitted with oars in case manpower was needed.

The chronicles of St. Brendan's voyage are explicit in details of the routes he took and the landfalls he made. However, the era of his exploits was the dark ages of Christianity when most people were illiterate and superstition and magic were used to spread the holy word. St. Brendan recorded his wanderings in parables that would impress the illiterate masses, citing fabulous beasts and mythical lands that would be worthy of his trials and his holy vocation.

According to one account, St. Brendan departed on his pilgrimage with shepherd's crook in hand and God's work in mind. He left Ireland about 650 A.D. and returned after a seven year voyage during which he encountered prayer singing birds, a lava breathing devil, and a wondrous whale. The friendly whale, which he named Jasconius, coiled himself like a snake around Brendan's curragh and carried them

The *Icelandic Map* drawn in 1570 by "cleric" scholars in Iceland, it clearly shows the lands discovered, explored, and settled by the Vikings. *Gronlandia* or Greenland, *Helleland* or Baffin Island, *Markland* or Labrador, and *Winlandia* or Newfoundland.

"in this manner for fourteen days" across the western Atlantic before bidding them adieu with an alfresco supper.

St. Brendan is also said to have encountered a fire-breathing dragon which he successfully overcame by imploring God to send "a large animal resembling a buck that burned like fire and threw the dragon into the air." On another occasion his small troop was threatened by a lava breathing devil which claimed, "If I dared before God, I could have you all killed and thrown into this fiery mass in revenge for the souls lost to me by your prayers." But again St. Brendan triumphed with his power of prayer.

After reaching the "Promised Land of the Saints," St. Brendan recorded that he found, "the ground golden and green from many precious stones...saw the most beautiful building with walls of gold and columns of carbuncle, the roof was of peacock feathers, and a fountain flowed rivers of milk and honey, wine and oil." After exploring the "Promised Land" for seven years, St. Brendan finally returned to Ireland with all but two of his crew, "one who was taken unto paradise and another who was taken by the devil"—apparently because he had stolen a necklace from a castle they had visited at their first landfall.

The lands he may have visited, however, are not so fabulous or mythical. The land of the "lava breathing devil" may well have been Iceland. Born of a volcano, even today it is noted for its hot springs and geysers and in St. Brendan's time it was in all likelihood even more active.

Viking voyagers three hundred years later recorded in their sagas that they found "Irish monks living in Iceland as hermits." From Iceland the Norsemen located Greenland and there were told by the Eskimos of strange men "dressed in white" whom they had encountered in lands of the west. The Vikings also encountered hermit monks in Greenland and recorded in their sagas that the friars told of an "Ireland the Great" that "lies away west in the ocean nigh to Vinland."

This information may have led the Vikings to believe that there was an even greater land beyond their *Greenland*. The Norsemen of Scandinavia, or Vikings as they have become popularly known, were pursuing a hot trail. The Irish or Celtic monks they followed had set out on a mission of mercy; the Vikings now set out on a mercenary mission.

The tales of the fabled "Ireland the Great," or the "Promised Land of the Saints," brought back to Greenland and Iceland by St. Brendan and his crew, left lingering stories with the hermit monks who remained there and were discovered by the voyaging Vikings. These stories probably spurred on the venturesome Norsemen who seemed to be insatiable in their thirst to discover and settle new lands.

In 985 A.D. Bjarni Herjolfsson decided to seek "Ireland the Great." He left his latest homeland, Greenland, on a voyage of exploration westward into uncharted waters. After several weeks he was driven off course in a severe storm and sighted land. Lost, and anxious to return home, he chose to return to Greenland and not make a landing. Upon his return he told of sighting a "new land" to the west and his story stirred the bold breast of an even braver Norseman, Leif Eiriksson.

Leif was the son of Eric the Red, a Viking outlaw who had been exiled from Iceland to Greenland for killing two men. Leif was to break with the family tradition and seek the new land purely out of curiosity, rather than being banished there for some crime. Since Herjolfsson had not explored the new land, Leif decided that he would. He bought a ship, enlisted a crew of thirty-five men and prepared for a voyage to "Ireland the Great."

In the year 1001 A.D. Leif "the Lucky" set sail on his voyage of discovery. Away to the west his course took him past Helluland (Flatland), Baffin Island, then Markland (Forested Land), Labrador, and finally Vinland (Wineland),

Newfoundland. Late that autumn Leif put his knarr into a quiet bay on the tip of the Great Northern Peninsula of Newfoundland at a place since named L'anse aux Meadows. The Norsemen passed a pleasant winter, the climate was mild, game was plentiful and the vast country seemed empty of people. In the spring the explorers packed up their cargo of timber and furs and sailed home to Greenland.

Once there, Leif told even more enthralling stories of "Wineland the good". His brother Thorvald decided to keep up the family tradition and further explore the "new-found-land". Thorvald borrowed his brother's ship, obtained his permission to stay at his settlement—which Leif had ambitiously named Leifsburdir—rounded up a crew of thirty-five men and sailed off to Vinland.

Thorvald spent two winters in the new world but he overstayed his welcome. In the second spring of his stay he sailed south along the east coast of the Great Northern Peninsula to further explore his brother's "discovery." In White Bay he encountered the natives of the island whom he called "skraelings."

The encounter was a bloody one, and Thorvald was killed and his body carried back to Greenland.

Despite the hostile encounter, other Norsemen followed the by now well charted route. In 1010 A.D. Thorfinn Karlsefni set out for Vinland with several ships, 150 would-be colonizers and "livestock of all kind" intent on establishing a permanent settlement in Wineland. He stayed two winters and succeeded in trading with the natives but the "skraelings" coveted the Norsemen's iron tools and weapons and a battle ensued which persuaded the Vikings to abandon their settlement in the "new world."

The Vikings continued their excursions to Vinland how-ever, perhaps for as long as two hundred years. The fish, furs and timber they found there and transported to Greenland seemed well worth the risks posed by the treacherous seas and the periodic attacks of hostile "skraelings."

Around this time another player joined the Norsemen's game, the climate. It began to change drastically in the north-ern regions as a mini ice-age enclosed the area, clogging the waterways westward and forcing the seal herds and fish stocks southward. Following the food sources were the Thule Eskimos of the Arctic, and Greenland became a hostile country where clashes between Norsemen and natives be-came common.

The Norse-Celtic settlers of Greenland, no longer the fierce, pillaging Viking voyagers they once had been, could not withstand the harsh climate and incessant attacks of the Eskimos. About 1300 A.D. they seemed to mysteriously dis-appear from Greenland. It is believed that those who did not perish straggled back to Iceland, or perhaps made their way to Newfoundland where they eventually died out.

By the late 1300s, knowledge of the Norsemen's at-tempts at settlement in the lands to the west was well known in the courts of northern European kingdoms of Norway, Denmark, Sweden and even England. For some time now Basque whalers from Northern Spain and southern France had been frequenting the northwest Atlantic as far as Iceland. Spurred on by the Icelandic reports of Greenland and Vin-land they ventured even farther northwestward in the wake of the Vikings.

As early as 1372 Spanish records show that Basque whalers were paying taxes to the Spanish crown on whales

Explorers of the "Age of Discovery" used primitave yet proven navigation aids: the sun, stars, and ocean currents.

they took in Labrador and Newfoundland waters. Some evidence suggests that Basque whalers had permanent fishing settlements in Newfoundland and Labrador a hundred years before Columbus or Cabot set out on their voyages of "discovery."

Columbus consulted Basque captains in the Azores a year before he made his voyage, and Cabot was also well acquainted with Basque sailors. He had made several voyages northward and along the coast of Africa and no doubt had encountered Basque skippers who had sailed to the northwest Atlantic.

About the year 1460, King Ferdinand I of Portugal petitioned Christian I, the king of Denmark-Norway, to make a joint expedition to the north Atlantic in search of a "Northwest Passage" to "Cathay." The two kingdoms seem to have had very cordial relations. The Portuguese had been trying for fifty years to find a southeast passage to China through or around Africa. Perhaps by 1460 they placed more credence in the Basque reports and Viking sagas from the north than in hopes of a passage to the south.

An expedition was agreed upon which saw two Portuguese noblemen, Joao Vaz Cortereal and Alvaro Martins Homen, accompany a Danish captain and a Norwegian pilot named John Scolvus, who had intimate knowledge of the northwestern Atlantic, sail westward from Iceland.

It is believed they sailed to Greenland then southward along the Labrador coast. In 1476 they reached Newfoundland, which the Portuguese Joao Vaz Cortereal named the Codfish country or "Terra do Bacalhao."

Upon their return to Portugal, the explorers gave a detailed account of their "discovery" which was widely circulated throughout the European courts. This expedition was probably the first unofficial voyage of discovery to the new world by European explorers. There no longer seemed any doubt that there was a "new world" to the west across the Atlantic.

And there was no shortage of anxious mariner men willing to "discover" it. In 1476, the same year as John Scolvus made his voyage, Christopher Columbus arrived in Portugal and the next year became a resident of that country. In Venice in 1476, John Cabot was receiving his citizenship in that city state after having been a resident there for fifteen years. The "age of discovery" had begun.

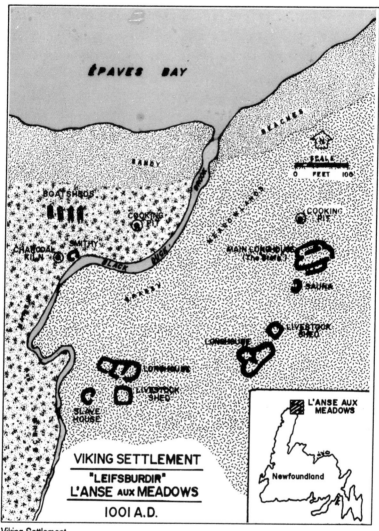

ÉPAVES BAY

BEACHES

SANDY

BOAT SHEDS

COOKING PIT

SMITHY

CHARCOAL KILN

BLACK DUCK

MEADOW MANOR

COOKING PIT

MAIN LONGHOUSE (The Smith)

SAUNA

BLACK DUCK

LIVESTOCK SHED

LONGHOUSE

LONGHOUSE

LIVESTOCK SHED

SLAVE HOUSE

SCALE
0   FEET   100

VIKING SETTLEMENT
"LEIFSBURDIR"
L'ANSE AUX MEADOWS
1001 A.D.

L'ANSE AUX MEADOWS

Newfoundland

Viking Settlement

Profile: L'Anse Aux Meadows—First settlement in the New-Found-Land.

WHEN THE ADVENTUROUS VIKING LEIF ERIKSSON landed in 1001 A.D. at a place that would later be called L'Anse aux Meadows, he found it to be a very likely site for a settlement. The wide deep bay had a long, sweeping beach in which Leif the Lucky and his thirty-five men could anchor their "knarr," grassy meadows for grazing their livestock, a fast stream for fresh water, and thick forests not far inland to supply them with wood for fuel and building materials. The Norsemen found the waters to be full of salmon and other fish and game in the form of caribou was plentiful in the hills nearby. Together with the grains and livestock, which included beef, mutton and pork, they were assured of plenty of food.

The Vikings prowled and explored the Atlantic in their swift, seaworthy longships.

Leif and his company first set about building their longhouses; wood framed structures enclosed by four foot thick sod or peat walls. The chief structure of the settlement was the "stofa." The largest and most communal of the buildings, it had several rooms including a kitchen, dairy room, three or four bedrooms, and if Leif had any women along there would have been a "lower" or women's room. Pits were dug along the long central fire place and lined with furs to become beds. The first white settlers in the new world spent a relatively comfortable and plentiful winter.

In the spring they loaded their knarrs with a cargo of wood, furs, fish and other samples of the land's bounty and returned to Greenland. Excited by Leif's success, his young brother Thorvald decided to try his luck. It took him a few years to convince thirty people to accompany him for a prolonged stay at Leifsburdir, as his brother had ambitiously named his settlement at L'Anse aux Meadows. In 1006 A.D. he left Greenland with enough provisions and livestock to sustain a long stay.

Thorvald repaired the longhouses at L'Anse aux Meadows and added a few outbuildings. He and his men spent a comfortable and uneventful winter and in the spring sailed south to explore the new land. In the bottom of White Bay they came across the first natives of the new world, the Beothuck Indians. The encounter turned out to be hostile. A fierce retaliation by the redmen saw Thorvald killed and his shaken colonizers made a hasty departure from Leifsburdir to Greenland.

The colonizers' reports of the savage "skraelings," as the Vikings named the Indians, left many would-be settlers wanting to stay in Greenland, but one successful and daunt-

Reconstructed Viking stofa and outbuildings at L'Anse aux Meadows.

less explorer-trader named Thorfinn Karlsefni was determined to try to make "Vinland" a further outpost of Norse settlement. He prepared a large expedition of sixty men, five women, and a large herd of pigs, sheep and cattle for an indefinite stay in the new land.

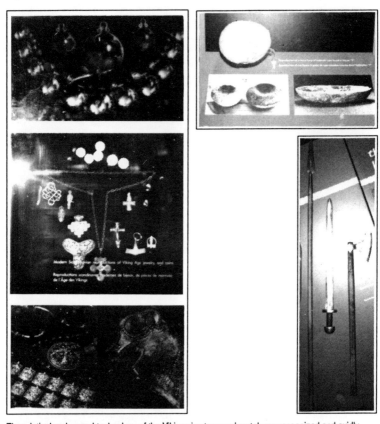

The relatively advanced technology of the Vikings in stone and metal was recognized and avidly sought after by the primitive Beothucks.

Karlsefni arrived at L'Anse aux Meadows in the fall, set the longhouses in order, added a couple of smaller houses to the settlement and settled in for the winter. Early the next summer a large party of Indians came to the settlement. After some initial confusion the Indians and whites carried on a lengthy bartering and trading session which saw the Indians trade huge piles of furs for bowls of milk and pieces of red cloth which they greedily sought.

It was the only visit from the Indians, and the Norsemen passed a quiet winter. They saw no more sign of the Indians until the following fall when they paid another visit to the white settlement. This time the Skraelings were not merely satisfied with milk and cloths. When one of them tried to steal some weapons he was killed and a fierce battle ensued that saw great losses on both sides. Karlsefni, fearful of further attacks, abandoned his attempt at settlement and returned to Greenland.

Some who left with him were determined to go back to Vinland. One of them, a woman named Freydis, concocted a scheme to claim Leifsburdir for herself. She struck a partnership with a pair of Norwegian brothers that would see both factions go to Vinland, work together and share in the profits of the voyage. After a winter of hunting, trapping and wood cutting, Freydis had all the Norwegian faction murdered. Then she took both cargoes and both ships and returned to Greenland claiming that the Norwegians had all been killed by the Skraelings.

There were other voyages to Vinland, some believe on and off for as long as two hundred years. It is thought that remnants of the Norse colonies in Greenland, fleeing advancing polar icefields and hostile Eskimos, may have fled to Vinland where they met a fate at the hands of the Skraelings like the one they'd hoped to escape. Perhaps it was merely the harsh climate that defeated the hearty Norsemen, but it is more likely that the wars fought later between whiteman and redman had been fought five hundred years earlier on a much smaller scale, but with one crucial difference: the redmen had won.

Two

Cabot's Destiny

M<small>ARCO</small> P<small>OLO</small> began the "age of discovery." Returning from a twenty-four year odessy to the far east, or "Cathay," in 1295 he told of the vast wealth to be found in spices and silks from the Orient. By 1300 A.D., his book *Description of the World*, had been read in all corners of Europe and triggered the search for a sea route to the oriental riches that would take only months compared to years overland.

Polo's reports enthused the rulers of seacoast kingdoms, especially those of Spain and Portugal. By now, enlightened Europeans believed that the world was indeed round. The "great circle" theory of navigation advanced by Cardinal Pierre d'Ailly, and supported by minds like Aristotle and Toscinelli, believed that the east could be reached by sailing west. From the city states of what would later become Italy, such as Venice, Genoa, and Milan, came the adventurous mariners, two of whom would become famous for their "discoveries" of the "new world."

John Cabot and Christopher Columbus were both born in the city of Genoa about the year 1450. There may have been two or three years difference in their ages but it is speculated that they grew up together and very possibly were boyhood

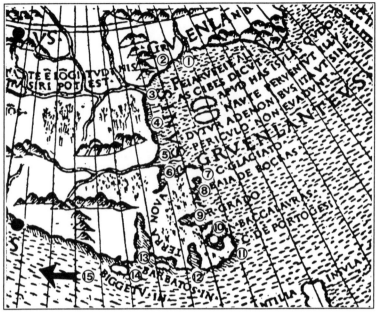

The Ruysch Map of 1508: Early explorers believed Greenland to be a part of North America. Looking for a passage to "Cathay" they discounted deep straits and inlets as mere bays or fiords. Thick ice was also a deterrence which prevented further exploration. Compared to maps of today, we may conjecture that features on the Ruysch Map correspond crudely with today's features. 1. Davis Strait. 2. Baffin Island. 3. Hudson Strait. 4. Labrador. 5. Groswater Bay or Hamilton Inlet. 6. Strait of Belle Isle. 7. Cape Bauld, (C. Glaciato). 8. Notre Dame Bay, (Baia De Rockas). 9. Gander Bay, (R. Grado). 10. Baccalieu Island, (In. Baccalavras). 11. Cape Race, (C. De Portugesi). 12. Placentia Bay. 13. Gulf of St. Lawrence. 14. Cape Breton or Nova Scotia. 15. The "Passage to Cathay."

friends. For such an accomplished person, very little can be pieced together definitely to tell us who John Cabot was. Even his name is uncertain. Cabot is an English corruption of the Genoese or Italian, which may have been any one of various forms such as Cabotto, Kaborta, Chiaboto, Bagoto, Cabuto, or several others which simply mean "Coaster"— one who engages in coastal shipping.

John Cabot was the son of a Genoese merchant named Egidus or Guilo Caboto who moved his family to Venice

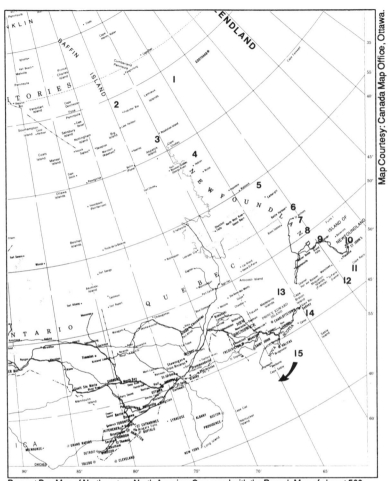

Present Day Map of Northeastern North America: Compared with the Ruysch Map of almost 500
years ago it can be seen that many land and sea features have a crude similarity.

when John was ten years old. In 1476, after fifteen years'
residence in the city state, Cabot was granted citizenship.
Four years later he married a Venetian woman whose name
was Mattea. By 1484 he had a family of three sons: Lewis,
Sebastion, and Sancius.

During this time, Cabot is believed to have been employed in several enterprises, among them geographer, merchant and real estate agent. From 1484-1494 he made several journeys as a merchant's agent to the middle east, whether overland or by sea is not certain, and is known to have visited Mecca where he encountered the spice caravans from the far east. There he made inquiries of the spice trade and formulated the theory that if the far east, or China, had a north-south coastline it could be reached more quickly by sailing westward rather than eastward.

Through his periodic voyages in the Mediterranean and along the coast of Africa, Cabot earned himself the reputation of being a "most skillful mariner" and an accomplished geographer. He knew from his contacts with middle east caravans that "Cathay" was not to be soon reached by sailing as the Portuguese had been trying for nearly fifty years from the east. He was convinced that the east could be reached more quickly by sailing towards the west.

However, as he raised his young family in Venice he busied himself as a real estate agent to make his daily bread. He bought and sold property, including houses, meadow lands and saltworks between 1482-84. During this time there seemed to be some dispute about his wife's dowry of seventy-five ducats which Cabot borrowed for some enterprise, giving her in return rights to his personal property consisting of a house and three saltworks which were to be returned to his heirs, presumably his sons, once he had repaid the dowry to his wife.

Cabot spent the years between 1485-90 in ventures to and from Mecca, where he became convinced that the shortest route to the Orient was westward across the Atlantic

The "Lopes Map"

and not eastward across the Indian Ocean. His convictions lured him ever westward where he knew both the Spanish and Portuguese were avidly engaged in looking for a passage eastward to "Cathay."

By 1490, it is likely that Cabot was living in Valencia, Spain. The King of Spain was approached in 1492 by a man identified as Johan Caboto, the Venetian, who had been residing in Valencia for two years, about constructing a harbour project in the city that would see it become a major Spanish port.

King Ferdinand wrote his Governor-General of Valencia, don Diego de Torre, on September 27th, 1492 about the proposed port project to be constructed on the beaches of his city.

"To our noble and beloved Councillor, Chamberlain and Governor-General in the Kingdom of Valencia, don Diego de Torre:

The King.

Chamberlain and Governor-General, we have been informed by Johan Caboto Montecalunya, The Venetian, that he arrived at this city two years ago, and during this time he has considered whether on the beach of this city a port could be constructed very easily both on land and sea, he has designed and painted plans of them, and he has brought them to us; and...it appears to us that...it would be something which would result in a great benefit for the common wealth of this kingdom; and...we have decided that some people who know of these things...should diligently examine whether the said Johan Caboto's statement is true as he has related it here....for if the aforesaid things could be done as easily as he says...."

In September and November of 1492 Cabot had meetings with King Ferdinand and outlined his plans, presenting the sovereign with elaborate drawings of his proposal. The King was favourably impressed but awaited evaluation from his Governor-General in Valencia.

In February of 1493 Diego de Torre replied to his highness, stating that in his opinion the port could not be constructed economically given Cabot's plans. He advised the king that unless the Venetian came up with some matching funds the expense to the Crown would be unreasonable.

Cabot could not find financial backing and in March, 1493 he was informed that his proposed project had been denied. Close on the heels of this news Cabot learned that Columbus had returned to Spain from his "voyage of discovery" to the west. News hailed that the "Admiral of the Ocean Sea" had found islands off the mainland of Asia and espied the continent of "Cathay" itself. Through March of 1493, the "Lord Grand Admiral," as Columbus was being called in the courts of Lisbon, travelled throughout Portugal then journeyed east to Seville and Barcelona to pay his respects to King Ferdinand of Spain. In April he passed through Valenica where John Cabot was still residing.

The two boyhood friends may have met and had long discussions about Columbus' voyage. The now famous Genoese had brought back richly clad servants and sailors, captured natives decorated in gold ornaments, and colourful parrots from Hispanola. Columbus professed, at least overtly, that he had reached Asia but he must have known, if he was familiar with Marco Polo's exploits, as he undoubtedly was, that the people and parrots he returned with were not from Asia. King Ferdinand was not about to admit to the

This Portuguese map, dated 1502, was quickly drawn after the voyages of the Correals. It clearly shows Newfoundland "Terra del Rey de Portugall" as being the discovery and propery of the King of Portugal.

world that his "Grand Admiral" had been unsuccessful in such a grandiose and expensive venture.

What Cabot may or may not have learned from Columbus is unknown. What is known is that the political intrigue of the times was, to say the least, convoluted. England had just concluded the Hundred Years' War with France, Spain was rattling sabres with France, Portugal and Spain were envious of one another, having been recently forced by the Vatican to become dual kingdoms. The Pope's edicts dictated to all these kingdoms, which were all Catholic at this time, and still struggling to recover from the catastrophe and costs of the crusades and private wars.

Cabot next decided to entreat the Kings of Spain and Portugal to sponsor him on a voyage of discovery across the northwest Atlantic, given that Columbus had not found one via the southern passage. Spain would not admit that its "Grand Admiral" had not found "Cathay" and Portugal was too stubborn to give up its search to find a southern passage through or around Africa. It then occurred to Cabot that England, the poor yet determined cousin of Europe, isolated and with contacts in Iceland, might well be the realm to back his ambitious venture.

While visiting the royal courts of Lisbon and Seville, Cabot became acquainted with English merchants, particularly those from Bristol who expressed steadfast interest in finding a northern route to Asia across the Atlantic Ocean. Given the political intrigue of the times, when spies were everywhere, or at least thought to be, Bristol merchants were surreptitious in their dealings with the Courts of Spain and Portugal. They were anxious, however, to find experienced mariners whom they could interest in pursuing their agenda in the North Atlantic.

Cabot may have been such a find. His reputation as a "skillful mariner" and geographer was well known and they may have lured Cabot to England with promises that they could interest Henry VII in Cabot's proposals. The merchants of Bristol had been outfitting expeditions to the westward for ten years by now and were looked upon favourably by the King who had visited them in 1480. Henry was interested in their ventures but being parsimonious, and with his royal coffers depleted by the Hundred Years' War with France, he was not too eager to embark on any costly expeditions.

It is likely that John Cabot journeyed to England in 1493 or 1494 at the behest of Bristol envoys in Spain or Portugal. There he found a large community of Italian merchants and money lenders who had connections with the Bristol merchants in Lisbon and Seville. By this time Cabot's reputation was well known and he was found to be a willing adventurer.

It was well known in the courts of Lisbon and Barcelona that the Bristol merchants had made a "voyage of discovery" to the west in 1480. Indeed, the Portuguese had co-operated with the Danish-Norway King Christian I in 1476 on a voyage of exploration. Exactly what the Bristol merchants had discovered remained a foggy disclosure which probably prompted the Iberian sovereigns to opt for a more southern route, thus the backing for Columbus' voyage.

The Bristol merchants were pursuing a brisk trade with Iceland by 1490 and a year later made an unsuccessful voyage towards the west in the wake of the Vikings. In 1492 it is thought they sponsored a second voyage to the west which saw them re-discover Labrador and make landfall at

Hamilton Inlet, on June 29th, 115 days before Columbus discovered central America, or Hispanola. A year later it is believed they sighted Newfoundland in the area of Cape Freels and the following year sailed past the island towards the Gulf of St. Lawrence where they discovered Cape Breton.

In 1495-1496 it is believed the Bristol voyagers sailed south along the coast of Newfoundland as far west as Bay St. George. Some think this may have been Cabot's first and undiscovered voyage to Newfoundland. It is known that Cabot was in England by 1495 and possibly a year earlier, living in Bristol where he had the ear of the English merchants who were busy looking for their own route to the spicelands of the Orient. A letter from John Day to the "Lord Grand Admiral," Christopher Columbus, tells of an abortive voayage made by John Cabot in 1495-1496.

In 1497, John Cabot would make an official and historic voyage to the "new-found-land."

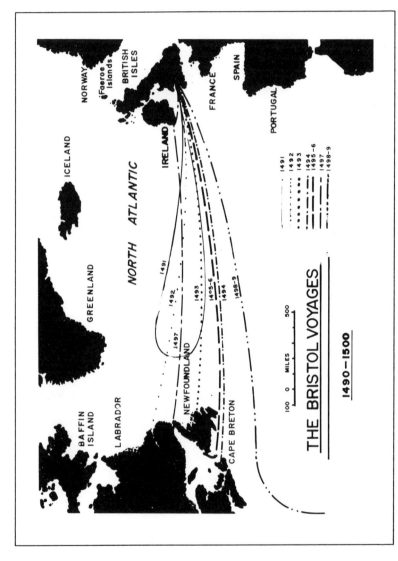

Map of the Bristol Voyages

Profile: Bristol: "Merchant Princes" Capitol

BRISTOL, ENGLAND, was one of the most prosperous and successful trading centres of the British kingdom, indeed of all northwestern Europe for over four centuries. It was the proud home of "merchant princes" who made incredible wealth, great minds who revolutionized men's thinking, and courageous explorers and colonizers who discovered and settled a "new world."

"Brygstowe," as it was originally named, was founded in the Middle Ages by Saxons who picked the site because of its difficult access and strategic position for defense. Located on the Avon River at its junction with the Frome River, it was eight miles inland from the Severn estuary and therefore safe from surprise attacks by marauding sea pirates. There the Saxons built a small town on a tiny peninsula and built a bridge from it across the Avon to the mainland. They named their new town "Brygstore" which simply meant "Place of the Bridge." It eventually became corrupted to "Bristowe" and then to Bristol which it remains today.

The Avon River, to which the city owed its security and wealth was a narrow, twisting and torturous waterway. It was lined with narrow, deep rocky gorges and rushed by tremendous tides that rose and fell quickly as much as twenty feet with powerful force behind them. These tides are believed to be the second highest and fastest in the world, second only to those of the Bay of Fundy.

In the centuries before the arrival of John Cabot and the discovery that would change the world, Bristol had become the most prosperous and important trading centre in West Country England, second only to London in all of Britain. Its geographic position on the west coast of the island and its

The central part of Bristol around 1675. Above is the Frome River with one of the old town's finer churches, St. Steeven's (sic.) on the west bank of the river just below the "Frome Bridge." Below is the Avon River and "The Bridge" after which the Saxons named the town "Brygstowe" in the Middle Ages. The original town was that part between the two rivers and left of "High Street" and the two river bridges. As the town grew it was forced to expand east and west across the two rivers and south, to the right of "High Street" and the two bridges.

City of Bristol Archives; Bristol, England.

relatively southerly location made it the "middle man" in the trade routes between northern and southern countries. To the north lay Ireland, Scotland and Iceland, and to the south the Iberian peninsula with Spain and Portugal. It traded English woolen goods; hats, caps, socks, yardcloth and blankets—Bristol was, in fact, home of the Blanket family who invented that utilitarian item. These good were traded to the north for dried codfish, and to the south for wine and olive oil. It also had a brisk trade with Bordeaux and Gascony in France, bartering its famous English woolens for "woad" a plant that was used to make a blue dye to colour their yardcloths.

By the mid 1400s the Bristolians were making their own voyages to further their trading ventures. They were convinced they could find new lands to the west and thus increase their trading wealth. Having heard the tales of St. Brendan they were determined to find his fabled lands, for as they put it, if a feeble monk in a flimsy "curragh" could voyage westward then they certainly could in a stout wooden vessel that was built "shipshape and Bristol fashion," a phrase that would be known around the world in 1497 after John Cabot did it.

At the end of the fifteenth century Bristol was a booming town of 10,000 people importing about £2500 worth of woad and 800 tons of wine, and exporting about 2200 "cloths," a "cloth" being twenty-four yards long. The Bristol merchants were shrewd business men who kept their profits in their own pockets by building their own ships and hiring their own captains. Their prosperity was also due in a large part to their favour with Henry VII. The King had granted them exemptions from certain dues and fees, and granted them their own Admiralty jurisdiction with the promise from the merchants that the Crown would share in any fortunes the Bristolians would make.

After the discovery of the new world, Bristol added North America to its list of trading partners, sending its famous English woolens across the Atlantic in exchange for cocoa and tobacco. Its ship building industry also greatly increased. They were determined and well capable of eliminating the "middle man" in their trading ventures. Indeed, Bristol's shipbuilding industry remained famous for centuries. Much later, the first English iron steamship, the *Great Britain* was built there.

Around 1600 the principal merchants of Bristol along with Sir Francis Bacon, Lord Chancellor of England, formed the London and Bristol Co. with the aim of establishing colonies in Newfoundland for the purposes of trade. In 1610 they sent John Guy, a native of Bristol, to establish a colony at Cupids. Despite precarious beginnings, it survived. Its founder returned to Bristol two years later where he became mayor of the rich city.

Other famous sons that the trading city claims include William Canyngnes, called England's first "merchant prince," who owned ten ships and used much of his great wealth to build the famous St. Mary's Redcliff cathedral in Bristol, and John Wesley, the founder of Methodism. It even claims the distinction of having the new world named for one of its sons, Richard Amerike, who was one of Cabot's backers and is buried there, denying the claim of others that the western hemisphere was named for Amerigo Vespucci.

The trading connection the London and Bristol Co. established with Newfoundland lasted three hundred years, gradually declining from having 100% of the Newfoundland trade in 1610 to 50% in 1875, and flickering to a mere 15% by about 1910, the Tercentenary of its founding of Guy's colony at Cupids.

The "Custom House" on the Avon River in Bristol where the "merchant princes" planned their schemes for wealth and counted the coins that piled up in their coffers.

Although trading links between the old "merchant prince" city and its oldest colony had all but disappeared, other links between them had not. In 1897, on the 400th anniversary of Cabot's discovery of Newfoundland, both Bristol and St. John's erected memorials to Cabot's feat. Cabot Tower was built on Signal Hill in St. John's and another Cabot Tower was built on Brandon Hill in Bristol to commemorate the courageous voyage of a man who belonged to neither but is claimed and beloved by both as their most famous son.

Three

Cabot's Discovery

K<small>ING</small> H<small>ENRY</small> VII of England had become interested in the proposals of the Bristol merchants after hearing about their voyages of venture in 1480 and 1481. In 1486, a year after he had become king, he visited the mercantile centre. Doubtless he discussed their early voyages and listened to their plans for future ones. But he could not be convinced to sponsor any of their future plans.

This changed in 1493 when he received news of Columbus' voyage. King Henry had been approached by Columbus about the venture of discovering the "new world" but the English monarch, busy trying to conclude a treaty with France and perhaps too poor to support such a risky venture, had dallied in his response to the Venetian who then sought the support of the royal Court of Spain. King Ferdinand and Queen Isabella were quicker to respond and King Henry could only have been disappointed in his lack of vision. In 1494 he visited Bristol once again and met with the merchant princes.

After the triumphant return of Columbus and the news of his "discovery," Henry was said to have commented that it was "a thing more divine than human to sail by the West to

The "Lord Grand Admiral"—
Christopher Columbus

the East." He was determined not to miss the boat, so to speak, a second time. He listened to Cabot's theories of finding a northern or mid-Atlantic route to the rich spice lands of the Orient, and to the propositions of the Bristol merchants that they would gain a monopoly on the spice trade in western Europe, in which the Crown would gain a "royal" share of the profits.

King Henry was impressed enough by the Venetian mariner's theories, and intrigued enough by the proposals of the merchants, who gave Cabot glowing recommendations as a "most skillful mariner," that he employed Cabot to negotiate trade treaties with Denmark-Norway concerning commerce with Iceland. Cabot had some success, for the following year the Bristol merchants petitioned the King to grant them letters patents to explore, claim and establish trade in lands not yet claimed by other countries.

The Bristol "merchant princes" were interested in Cabot's theory and hoped it could be proven true. However, they were also interested in exploiting new fishing grounds. Their reliance on Iceland for their supply of "stockfish," or salt cod, was proving to be more unreliable and troublesome in recent years. This was partly due to the brawls that resulted when English sailors visited Icelandic ports, and partly due to the interference of the Hanseatic League in their trade relations with the isolated North Atlantic island. The Icelanders knew where the fish stocks were and the Bristolians had thought they'd found them on a couple of occasions but had no proven route to them. They hoped that Cabot, as a skillful mariner and competent geographer, could map the route for them. Cabot, for his part, was willing to locate their fishing grounds for them if they were willing to back his goal of finding the route to "Cathay."

The Icelanders were secretive about what their Viking forefathers had discovered, which may be why they survived as such an isolated colony of commerce. The Bristol merchants knew they had discovered an extensive land across the Atlantic in roughly the same latitude as England. They believed it to be the Vinland of the Vikings and believed the Icelanders had a proven route to it which accounted for their great success in the fishery. If they could chart a proven route to it, they could eliminate the Icelanders in the salt cod trade.

Cabot convinced the Bristolians that they had found the northern coast of Cathay, northern China, and that if it had a north-south coastline he could, by coasting south and west, find a north Atlantic or mid-Atlantic passage to the rich cities of China and "Cipango," or Japan, as recorded by Marco Polo. The Venetian was convinced that Columbus had not found Cathay, especially after his second voyage in 1494. Columbus was still exploring "Hispanola," the Caribbean Islands, and Cuba, having not yet reached the mainland of South America where the gold of the Aztecs, Mayans, and Incas would be found. Columbus' crews returned from the 1494 voayge grumbling about the hot as hell climate, poor savages and lack of riches to be found in Columbus' "new world." The mutual admiration and persuasion society of Bristol merchants and Cabotian explorers had come to an agreement.

In 1495, the merchants of Bristol petitioned the King with their proposal to make England rich:

"To the king, our sovereigne Lord. Please it your Highness of your most noble and habundant grace to grant unto John Cabotto citizen of Venes, Lewes, Sebastyan and Sancto his sonnes your gracious letters patents under your grete sele in due forme to be made according to the tenour hereafter ensuying...(the draft of the charter is lost).....and they shall during their lyves pray God for the prosperous continuance of your most noble and Royale Estate, long to enduer."

Henry VII was anxious. After Columbus' initial success, his further explorations had been fruitless in finding the western passage to Cathay. The venture proposed by Cabot could be the panacea England needed to shed its "poor cousin" image within the European community. But Henry had a problem. Following the discovery by Columbus, Spain and Portugal became embroiled in a controversy over who should be sailing where. After a year of bickering between the two Iberian kingdoms, the Pope, Spanish born Alexander VI, decreed that a line, called the "linea divisionis," be drawn on the world map that would see everything east of it be the provenance of Portugal and everything west of it belong to Spain.

When this line was drawn, geographers erroneously placed it a full 20° longitude east of where it should have been. When this mistake was discovered and corrected the "linea divisionis" place the "Terra do Baccalaos" in the realm of the Portuguese about the year 1500. It was the same line extended southward that gave Brazil to Portugal, the only Portuguese colony in the new world. All the remainder of South America, Central America, Mexico and a great part of the United States were all Spanish territory.

But in 1495, all this was yet to be discovered. The dual Iberian kingdoms were busy southeast and southwest of their boundaries and Henry considered the north Atlantic "no-man's" land. He decided to pursue his venture, ignoring the papal bull which had politely suggested that he keep out of continental Christian affairs. What the Bristol merchants wanted of him was an official letters patent that would legally support them in the event of any protests from Spain or Portugal. Henry, perhaps a little peeved by the Pope's patronage, decided he would grant it.

The rivalries and jealousies of the European kingdoms at the time were more than paranoia. Spain was at that time preparing to go to war with France and was counting on support from England, since England and France had long been enemies. But Spain heard of the Bristol merchant-Cabot explorer venture before Henry VII had even given official sanction to it. On January 21, 1496, Gonsalez de Puebla, Spanish ambassador in England, wrote Ferdinand and Isabella a report informing the sovereigns of King Henry's intentions. On March 28th, the Spanish royalty replied..."In regard to what you say of the arrival there of one like Columbus for the purpose of inducing the King of England to enter upon another undertaking like that of the Indies, without prejudice to Spain or to Portugal, if the King aids him as he has us, the Indies will be well rid of the man." This facetious comment by the Spanish sovereigns, if Henry ever heard it, would have done little to endear him to his haughty "allies."

On March 5th, 1496, Henry VII of England granted a letters patent to John Cabot to discover and claim a "new world."

> "Henry by the grace of God, king of England and France, and lord of Ireland, to all whom these presents shall come. Greeting.
>
> Be it knowen that we have given and granted, and by these presents do give and grant for us and our heires, to our wellbeloved John Cabot citizen of Venice, to Lewis, Sebastian and Santus, sonnes of the sayd John, and to the heires of them, and every of them, and their deputies, full and free authority, leave, and power to saile to all parts, countreys and seas of the East, of the West, and of the North, under our banners and ensigns, with five ships of what burthen or quantity soever they be..., to seeke out, discover, and finde whatsoever isles, countreys, regions or provinces of the heathen and infidels whatsoever they be...."

John Cabot and his sons were required to pay "as often as they shall arrive at our port of Bristol...to pay to us in wares or money the fifth part of the capitall gaine so gotten." The letters patent also stipulated that they were "bound and holden only to arrive" at the port of Bristol. They were to be "free from all paying of customes," and it was decreed that any territories Cabot discovered "may not of any other of our subjects be frequented or visited without the licence of the aforesayd John and his sonnes, and their deputies." The Letters patent belaboured the fact that Cabot's venture was to be solely his, his sons and heirs, and their "deputies," which meant the Bristol merchants. As their agent, Cabot was being granted the singular right to exploit any lands and resources he might find. It seems a good deal had been struck all around.

Cabot got the opportunity to pursue his dream of reaching Cathay and Cipango, the Bristol merchants would only be the shippers and receivers of any cargoes, landing them without customs or duties, and Henry VII would receive a fifth of all the profits without having to spend one penny on the expedition.

What Cabot, and indeed everyone else of his time did not know, was that those who had proposed the theory of circumnavigation had under-estimated the circumference of the earth by about 7,000 miles. They did not know that within this area there was a completely "new world," and beyond that another vast ocean—the Pacific. Explorers like Columbus and Cabot believed they could reach the east by sailing west. They believed the lands they encountered were some fabled, large island as Hy-Brasil or Antille and that there was surely a way around them to the riches of the Orient. Again, they could not know that the western hemisphere was a contiguous land mass from the Arctic Circle to Antarctica save for the two passages at the very extremities of the hemisphere; the "Northwest Passage" and the "Drake Passage."

The unknown did not deter Cabot and his "deputies." Their Letters patent had been issued only a couple of months when they had their expedition prepared. The voyage was unsuccessful. The only report of it was made to the Spanish by an Englishman, John Day, who had business interests in that country. He told that "Cabot went with one ship, his crew confused him, he was short of food, and ran into bad weather, and he decided to turn back." Day was being politic when he said that Cabot's "crew confused him." Cabot's crew were Bristol seamen, accustomed to following the "Icelandic route" via Iceland, Greenalnd, Baffin Island and Labrador to "Vinland." They probably thought Cabot's course, sailing due west from Ireland to "Vinland," was too far south. In all likelihood there was a confrontation, if not outright mutiny, that forced Cabot to return to Bristol.

Little was reported about the aborted voyage, probably because the Bristol merchants did not want to have King Henry reassess his commitment. Cabot's Bristol backers hurriedly put together an expedition for the following year. By May of 1497 they were ready.

Cabot was given command of a new ship, probably built in Bristol by its expert shipbuilders, and christened by Cabot himself, the *Matthew* after his Venetian wife Mattea. His ship was a small vessel, built to be seaworthy and fast. Fashioned after the "navicula" trading ships of the Mediterranean it was capable of carrying only about fifty tons cargo and a crew of twenty men. Different accounts give Cabot's crew as being either a full complement of twenty or being just shy at eighteen. It consisted of two Bristol merchants, about fourteen hearty Bristol sailors, and two personal friends, one a Genoese and the other a Bergundian who was a barber. The barber was probably brought along to act as a medic, a role often filled by barbers in those days when doctors and surgeons were few. The names of the two merchants are not known for certain, but they may have been Michael Thorne and Hugh Eliot, two "deputies" of Cabot who later inherited

The Start of the voyage that discovered Newfoundland
Departure of John and Sebastian Cabot from Bristol, 1497

Cabot's letters patent of 1496. Well respected and feared by the Bristol sailors, they went along on the voyage to ensure that there was no "disagreement" with Cabot as there had been on the 1496 escapade.

On May 20th, 1497, John Cabot and his family, along with crew of the tiny ship *Ye Matthew,* gathered in the stately church of St. Stephens on the banks of the Frome River in Bristol to pray for their successful and safe voyage. From the church they made their way to the docks on the Avon, where the ship and its crew were given a final blessing before departing on their voyage of exploration.

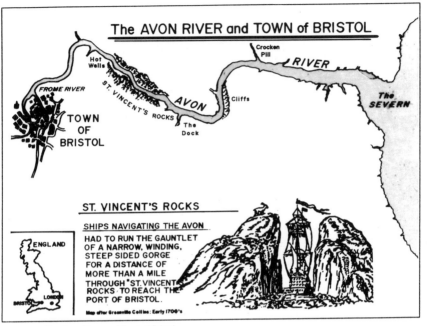

The Avon River and Town of Bristol

Ye Matthew then turned quietly down the Avon River, snaked past the "Hotwells" and gingerly through the "gorge" and St. Vincent's Rocks. Once safely around "Horseshoe Bend," the small ship put into the tiny village of Crocken Pill, where Cabot took on board a local river pilot named James George Ray. The pilot then took control of Cabot's vessel until it reached the mouth of the river and Avonmouth where Ray went ashore and Cabot continued westward along the estuary of the Severn into the Bristol Channel.

As he sailed west through the Bristol Channel watching for the south coast of Ireland on his starboard side, Cabot made his final preparations for his voyage westward. His mission was not intended to be a trading one. His small ship was barely large enough to contain its crew and the provisions they would need for an extended voyage, leaving little room for trade goods or any cargoes they might acquire as a result of bartering in China. Cabot's voyage was a reconnaissance, to ascertain that the Bristol explorers had found a mainland, which he was then to follow southwest to the rich cities of Cathay and Cipango, charting his course along the route. Any trading expeditions would be made by following voyages.

Cabot would not be sailing only by the age old methods that relied on the North Star, the sun, the wind directions and sea currents. As a believer in the "circle of navigation" theory, he was also a believer in the new scientific instruments of navigation. He was in all likelihood equipped with a quadrant, traverse tables and traverse board, a compass and dividers, sounding lead, a glass, a notebook of mathematical tables, and perhaps a magnetic dry-card compass and, even an astrolabe. He also proved his skill by being able to use them.

The explorer proposed to strike north to the southwest coast of Ireland and Dursey Head. That point was the most southwest point of the island, and from there he proposed to set his course westward on roughly 51° 30′ latitude and follow this "easting" westward to landfall. Dursey Head was a common jumping off point for Bristol voyagers who went west, but Cabot, using the scientific apparatus of navigation could set his course directly from the Bristol Channel and still have found Newfoundland. He may have sailed northerly to Ireland so that Spain would not get information that he was sailing south into waters claimed by that country.

From his talks with the Bristol sailors and his contacts with the Icelanders and Norwegians, Cabot had learned that late April and early to mid May usually offered easterly

The Discovery of Newfoundland
John Cabot in the *Matthew*, off Cape Bonavista, 1497

winds which would speed him on his way. The small, fast, maneuverable *Matthew* could take the wind on her beam and make as much as five or six knots. However, the ship probably did not enjoy such favourable winds, as it took her over four weeks to make landfall.

Although the weather was fair the hoped for easterly winds were not predominant. Cabot found himself battling northerlies and southerlies and was kept busy with his instruments trying to maintain his "easting" and stay on course. Once close to Newfoundland he most likely also encountered the floating ice pans and dense fog banks of the season that undoubtedly slowed his progress and put him a little off course. The explorer also noted about this time that his compass was reading about two "rhumbs" off north—a "rhumb" on old compasses being equal to about 11° on a modern compass. After "laying-to" and weathering the gale, Cabot corrected his course and on June 24th, 1497 heard the cry of "Land-ho"! from the crowsnest of *Ye Matthew*.

Sailors who had probably been grumbling for days about their "furriner" captain who had said the voyage would probably take only three weeks and had turned out to be more than four, now were no doubt ecstatic with the sight.

It was shortly after 5:00 A.M. when the "new-founde-land" was sighted. Through his telescope, Cabot surveyed the looming headland. He dubbed the sighted headland "Prima Tierra Vista,"—land first sighted. It has long been a controversy where that first sighted land was, but it was surely somewhere on the east coast of Newfoundland.

The sighting was made early, in a calm, clear morning and the landfall could be seen from as far as fifteen miles. Sailors felt lucky and relieved to sight land at such an early time of day, as it gave them a lot of time to work into a harbour. Cabot soon determined that the looming headland was too rough to approach for a landing and saw that a lower landmass stretching to the southwest looked more hospitable.

Later that morning, the feast of St. John the Baptist, Cabot named his "Prima Tierra Vista," land first sighted, as he made his chart notes and turned his course south along the stretching coastline ahead of him. Within a few hours he found a deep, sheltered harbour surrounded by high hills covered with thick forests of spruce and fir trees.

CABOT'S DISCOVERY

Cabot anchored the *Matthew*, lowered the ship's boat and with a small party rowed ashore. With all the pomp he could muster in a primitive setting he had a procession led up to the beach to "terra firma," where he planted a cross, and the banners of Henry VII, the Pope, and St. Mark, patron saint of Venice, presumably for sentimental reasons. He had formally taken possession for his sovereign, as per his Letters patent, of the "New Isle" as he named it.

Whether by design or accident, Cabot had landed at a site that had recently been occupied by natives. He reported finding "a trail that went inland, they saw a site where a fire had been made, they saw manure of animals which they thought to be farm animals, and they saw a stick half a yard long pierced at both ends, carved and painted with brasil, and by such signs they believe the land to be inhabited. Since he was with just a few people, he did not dare advance inland beyond the shooting distance of a crossbow, and after taking fresh water he returned to his ship." This report was phrased so as to put the best light on his discovery. The remark that he found "farm animals" was probably made to reassure chroniclers that he had made contact with the civilized, though infidel, inhabitants of Cathay who were the poor pastoral peasants of a rich kingdom.

The day was fine and hot, and Cabot may have believed, given his fervour to find Cathay, that it was a land where the fabled brasil-wood might grow and silkworms could be bred. Being in doubt, the Venetian explorer, as one chronicler put it, did nothing and returned to his ship.

Cabot and his "deputies" were a little apprehensive about having come across an inhabited camp site but not seeing any of the natives. The recently burning fire told them that whoever had been there had seen them first, and their swift disappearance made the Englishmen believe they would be hostile if encountered.

Back aboard the *Matthew*, Cabot checked his bearings. He took a meridional altitude of the sun, and dawn and evening sights on Polaris, the North Star, calculating that his position was on the approximate latitude of Dursey Head, Ireland at 50°37′ latitude.

Since it was early summer, the weather was fine and they were still well provisioned, Cabot's "deputies" decided that they could spend some time exploring the coastline that stretched far to the south of them.

Cabot and his crew may not have known it, but they were travelling in the wake of the Viking explorers who had proceeded them five hundred years earlier on almost exactly the same course.

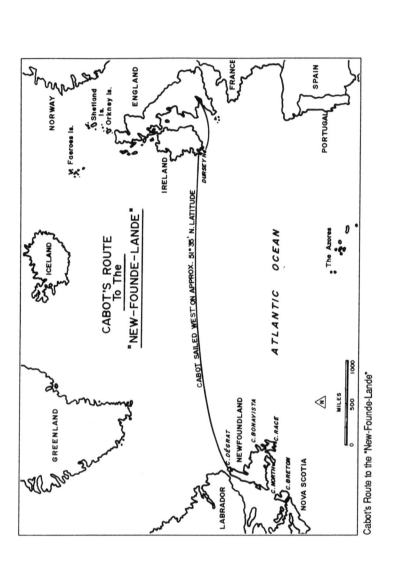

Cabot's Route to the "New-Founde-Lande"

Profile: *Ye Mathew*—Ship of Discovery

ON A CALM JUNE MORNING IN 1497, the small ship *Ye Mathew*, possibly sailing on her maiden voyage, sailed into the pages of history when her master, John Cabot, and his crew of nineteen sighted Newfoundland and became the "official" discoverers of North America.

Ye Mathew was a tiny ship, even when compared to its contempories. It had flat decks and three masts and was called a "navicula," better known in the Tudor times as a bark. Naviculas were a type of ship used mostly in the Mediterranean in the fourteenth to seventeenth centuries as a trading vessel. Though described by some as a "caravel," or a type of craft much used by the Spanish and English in later

Nfld. Museum, St. John's

Model of *Ye Mathew,* Cabot's ship which carried him to the "New-Found-Land.
Photo: B.D. Fardy

years for their voyages to the new world, it was distinct from the caravel class of ships.

Navicula is from the Latin term Navicularii, meaning shipper; the owner or supplier of goods being shipped. The "Naviculii," those who owned or shipped the goods, were always well insured by the Roman government who often supplied the ships and paid for any repairs to them. Fees charged by the Roman government often allowed for the "Naviculii" to receive a percentage of the value of their cargoes, which in some cases amounted to a staggering total of fifteen million bushels of wheat a year.

Ye Mathew was a fast, able and weatherly craft, proven by the fact that she made a several thousand mile voyage across the Atlantic and back in less than three months. Its three masts hoisted square sails on the fore and main, and lateen canvas on the mizzen. It was about sixty feet long and of "50 tons burthen," that is capable of carrying fifty tons of wine as its cargo, which was the measurement of a ship's capacity in the fifteenth century. It was an exquisitely crafted vessel with a deep waist, high forecastle and spacious sterncastle. Its size suggests that it would have a fathom draught, given its cargo capacity and crew size of eighteen to twenty men.

The ship was probably built by Bristol ship builders or purchased by Bristol merchants explicitly for John Cabot sometime after his arrival in England in 1494. Records of the Bristol Customs Office show no record of the vessel before 1496. Cabot christened the ship for his wife, a Venetian whose name was Mattea. In the Italian pronunciation of the name it sounded like Matthew to the English ear, and since they had

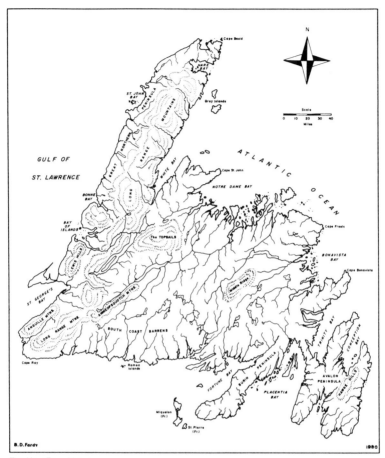

The New-Found-Land

no femine form of the name it was anglicized by the Bristol merchants to "Mathew."

After her return to England in 1497, *Ye Mathew* was pressed into other mercantile service. She did not sail with Cabot on his second voyage; if she had she would have been lost with her captain who disappeared during that voyage. Further records show that *Ye Mathew* was employed for several years after its historic voyage in shipping trade goods to and from England, Ireland, France and Spain, mastered by various Captains. Her length of service to the Bristol merchants lasted about fifteen years. Her final fate is unknown, but in 1513 the Bristol Customs recorded that the *New Mathew* was still in service.

A model of *Ye Mathew* constructed by local historians of Bristol and on display in the British Museum is based on the Hastings manuscript and is considered to be a very accurate and excellent one. Another replica, based on the Bristol model, is held by the Newfoundland Museum.

Ye Mathew was commemorated by Canada in 1990 by the arrival on December 1st, at St. John's of the fifty-one metre Canadian Hydrographic Survey Ship *Matthew*, which is in use as a scientific research vessel along the coasts of Newfoundland-Labrador.

"It is pleasant," one observer commented, "to think of John Cabot's compliment to his wife, perhaps the only wife of a great explorer to see her name borne by her husband's ship."

Four

Cabot's Exploration

ONCE LEAVING HIS LANDFALL, Cabot turned south, to coast
the straight shore of the great northern peninsula of Newfoundland. He soon recognized that the coastline was steep,
covered with dense forests and had few harbours that could
be safely entered. It is recorded that he did not land again
during his coastal exploration, which took almost a month
and covered about "300 leagues"—about 950 nautical miles.

The reasons that Cabot did not attempt another landing
are various as given by different observers. Some believe he
became "alarmed" by what he found at his first landing and
feared attack by hostile natives. Probably the most interesting explanation comes from Admiral S.E. Morrison, who
claimed that Cabot did not land a second time because of
"...the mosquitoes. The rocky surface of eastern Newfoundland is full of small depressions which catch and hold
the melting snow; swarms of mosquitoes breed therein and
make life miserable for all but the most hardened 'Newfies'."
A more likely explanation is that he simply wanted to chart
as much as possible of the coastline he had "discovered"
before his provisions ran short.

As he coasted south, Cabot saw the large looming coastline of northern Newfoundland. As his job was to do a reconnaissance survey he did not waste much time exploring the deep bays he encountered. He swept past White Bay and stayed well clear of the island dotted bay of Notre Dame. His course was to follow the outline of the land ahead of him, and once close to the shoreline, this course led him ever eastward and southward.

If he encountered fog, which he undoubtedly did, he may have had to land and wait for it to clear. He was close enough to the land at least one time when he reported that he saw: "...two forms running one after the other, but (Cabot) could not tell if they were human beings or animals; and it seemed to them that there were fields where they thought might also be villages, and they saw a forest whose foliage looked beautiful."

Cabot may have been sighting barren lands, or primary forests after a fire. In all likelihood they were a change from the dense forested lands he had been seeing on his cruise down the Northern Peninsula. At this time of year Notre Dame Bay and its offshore islands were heavily populated by the Beothuk Indians in pursuit of fish and birds to supplement their winter diet of caribou, and the landscape would be drastically different from what Cabot had been observing on his cruise down the Northern Peninsula.

As he drew into Notre Dame Bay he stayed clear of the numerous islands and crossed the wide bay to the looming landmass of Fogo Island. Skirting the island he turned southeast along the "straight shore" of Bonavista North. Rounding Cape Freels, he sailed across the island-dotted Bonavista Bay and turned south around Cape Bonavista. He may have ventured a short distance into Trinity Bay, but quickly turned north again, crossed Conception Bay and rounded Cape St. Francis on the Avalon Peninsula.

The explorer may have found the narrow entrance to St. John's harbour, and even have entered its sheltered waters. It is thought by some that he did, and thus the name of the

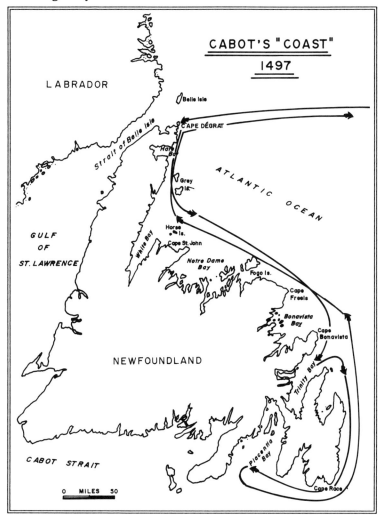

CABOT'S "COAST"
1497

LABRADOR

Belle Isle

CAPE DÉGRAT

Strait of Belle Isle

Hare Bay

Grey Is.

ATLANTIC OCEAN

GULF
OF
ST. LAWRENCE

White Bay

Horse Is.

Cape St. John

Notre Dame Bay

Fogo Is.

Cape Freels

Bonavista Bay

Cape Bonavista

NEWFOUNDLAND

Trinity Bay

CABOT STRAIT

Placentia Bay

Cape Race

0   MILES   50

island's capital today. From there, Cabot continued south along the southern shore to Cape Race, where he found his course turning due west.

He sailed across Trepassey Bay and sighted the 500 feet high headland of Cape St. Mary's. Passing into Placentia Bay he saw only the vast expanse of the Atlantic Ocean to his west and south. Had he proceeded a little farther he would have sighted the long Burin Peninsula, but as its landmass is relatively low lying and flat he did not see it from mid Placentia Bay and decided that the sea was wide and open far to the west.

Cabot now believed he had found the passage around the "Brasil" of legend and through to "Cathay." Since he was on a reconnaissance expedition, he now chose to turn around and retrace his route to his point of landing where he intended to pick up his "easting" and sail directly back to his point of departure, Dursey Head, Ireland.

The explorer may have been running low on provisions or his lead soundings, taken in the deep waters of Placentia Bay and showing no bottom at 100 fathoms, convinced him that he was in deep seas again and would not encounter any further land soon.

Retracing, or "doubling" his course as it is called, made a lot of navigational sense since it allowed Cabot to increase his knowledge of the coastline he had explored and allowed him to make further observations for his charts. Since he spent about a month in this endeavour he may have explored some of the bays he'd passed by on his southward route.

It was noted that on his return route to Cape Dégrat, he "saw two islands, but was unwilling to land, in order not to lose time, as he was in want of provisions." What these two islands were can only be speculated on. They may have been the small islands off the southern shore of the Avalon peninsula, but this is unlikely since they are so close to the mainland that they would not be remarkable. Cabot had passed dozens of such close lying islands in the other bays northwards. But on his return voyage to Cape Dégrat, he was staying closer to the shoreline, and may even have been investigating some of the deeper bays. It is probable that the islands he noted on his return trip were the Horse Islands off the Baie Verte peninsula, which he had widely skirted on his southward cruise and probably did not see because he was too far off shore or the islands were shrouded in fog.

Once he returned to Cape Dégrat on Quirpon Island at the tip of the great Northern peninsula, Cabot reset his "easting," this time keeping the North Star on his port side, and headed east to England. He left Cape Dégrat on about July 20th, and after a smooth and fast fifteen day voyage arrived in Brittany on August 4th.

Cabot's landfall on his return voyage to England was not where he set out to end up when he left Newfoundland. This has led many to believe that his navigation was not as good as some believe since his homeward landfall was at Ushant, in the Brittany Islands, a full 100 miles south of his intended destination. One contemporary chronicler reported that "he (Cabot) reached Brittany because the sailors confused him, saying that he was heading too far north."

Allowing that the *Mathew* sighted Ushant about daybreak on August 4th, she had only about 100 miles to travel due north to hit the British Channel. Cabot's crew now knew that they had been wrong, and also knew that they had two more days before reaching home. By dawn of August 5th, Cabot's ship had reached the Severn Estuary where he picked up familiar landmarks such as the Welsh mountains, Flatholme and Steepholme. By evening he had reached Avonsmouth and anchored in King's Road. Cabot next day began his ascent up the Avon. If he had a fair wind he might have made Crocken Pill, where he was probably towed around Horseshoe Bend and through the "gulch" and St. Vincent's Rocks by the stalwart rowers of the tiny village.

When the *Mathew* reached port in Bristol she was met by a throng of people who had received news of her arrival the day before. Families of the crew, excited onlookers, and the merchant princes and city fathers all gathered to welcome back the tiny vessel and hear the news of the discovery of the "New Isle" by Cabot. The ship was quickly cleared through the British Customs House and Cabot wasted no time in making his report to King Henry.

Cabot travelled the main road from Bristol to London on horseback, perhaps accompanied by his sons, stopping over two nights at traveller's inns, and making the 30 mile journey in three days. On the morning of August 10th, he rode to Westminster to see King Henry.

He brought back no treasures, silks or spices, or slaves, only news. Yet the English sovereign was well pleased. He paid Cabot £10 for his discovery of the "new-founde-lande," as Henry dubbed his newly acquired colony, and discussed with Cabot plans for another expedition the following year. The King promised to give Cabot "ten armed ships as he desires and has given him all the prisoners to be sent away, that they may go with him, (Cabot) as he has requested." It seems King Henry was intent on an extensive trading expedition and the inclusion of convict labour among the crews may have meant he intended to attempt to establish some kind of outpost or colony. Whatever the King's intention, his plans would have to wait. Henry had looming domestic problems which were to take precedence over everything else.

While Henry was away in the West Country putting down a revolt by Cornishmen and repelling an invading Scottish army, Cabot returned to Bristol to rejoin his wife and three sons. King Henry had given him a gift of £10 to spend on his family. This may seem paltry but it was a considerable amount for the fifteenth century.

In Bristol, Cabot spent his time walking about the town, with throngs of people always at his heels, listening to his stories of the "new isle," talking about the riches of the land and the bountiful seas, so rich with codfish that a weighted basket dropped overboard could be pulled back up in moments, and be overflowing with the large fish. This was very good news to the Bristol merchant princes. Now they could catch their own "stockfish" and cut out the troublesome Icelanders.

Foreign ambassadors reported all the fanfare to their sovereigns in their native lands . In August one wrote to his brother in Italy that Cabot "is called the Grand Admiral and vast honour is paid to him as he goes dressed in silk, and these English run after him like mad, and indeed he can enlist as many of them as he pleases, and a number of our rogues as well."

Another wrote of the importance Cabot had gained and his rising prominence in England with perhaps a taint of envy. "I have also spoke with a Bergundian," the Ambassador wrote, "one of Messer Zoane's (Cabot) companions,

John Cabot in Bristol after his voyage of "Discovery" to the "New-Founde-Land."

A Letter written at the time states: "Honours are heaping upon Cabot. He is called Grand Admiral, he is dressed in silk, and the English run after him like madmen."

who corroborates everything. He wants to go back, because the Admiral, which is the name they have given to Messer Zoane, has given him an island. He has given another to his barber, a Genoese by birth, and both consider themselves counts, while my lord the Admiral esteems himself a prince...As I have made friends with the Admiral, I might have an archbishopric if I chose to go there...."

These foreign ambassadors, who were little more than spies, sent to England to keep an eye and ear of King Henry's activities, also reported in great detail on Cabot's voyage and its results. Most of their reports reflected their authors' belief that Henry was planning to take over some of the territory that had been claimed by Spain and Portugal.

One report of Cabot's voyage was sent not by a foreign ambassador, but by an Englishman named John Day, who had some business dealings in Spain. Late in 1497, Day wrote the "Great Admiral" of Spain, Christopher Columbus himself, giving him great detail of Cabot's voyage. He also told of a globe and map Cabot had made of his voyage but the globe he could not trace and has since disappeared. Day obtained a copy of the map and is believed to have sent it to Columbus. It was further recopied to reflect Spanish interests and in subsequent years its original content became confused.

Day wrote;

"Thus your Lordship will know that the cape nearest to Ireland is 1800 miles of Dursey Head which is in Ireland, and the southernmost part of the Island of the Seven Cities is west of Bordeaux River, and your Lordship will know that he landed at only one spot of the mainland, near the place where the land was first sighted, and they disembarked there with a crucifix and raised banners with the arms of the Holy Father and those of the King of England, my master; and they found tall trees of the kind masts are made, and other smaller trees, and the country is very rich in grass. In that particular spot, as I told your Lordship, they found a trail that went inland, they saw a site where a fire had been made, they saw manure of animals, and they saw a stick half a yard long pierced at both ends, carved and painted with brasil and by such signs they believe the land to be inhabited. Since he was with just a few people, he did not dare advance inland beyond the shooting distance of a crossbow, and after taking in fresh water he returned to his ship. All along the coast they found many fish like those which in Iceland are dried in the open and sold in England and other countries, and these fish are called in English "stock-fish;" and thus following the shore they saw two forms running on land one after the other, but they could not tell if they were human beings or animals; and it seemed to them that there were fields where they thought might also be villages, and they saw a forest whose foliage looked beautiful. They left England toward the end of May, and must have been on the way 35 days before sighting land; the wind was east-north-east and the sea calm going and coming back, except for one day when he ran into a storm two or three days before finding land; and going so far out, his compass needle failed to point north and marked two rhumbs below. They spent about one month discovering the coast and from the above mentioned cape of the mainland which is nearest to Ireland, they returned to the coast of Europe in fifteen days. They had the wind behind them, and he reached Brittany because the sailors confused him, saying that he was heading too far north. From there he came to Bristol, and he went to see the King to report to him all the above mentioned; and the King granted him an annual pension of twenty pounds sterling to sustain himself until the time comes when more will be known of this business, since with God's help it is hoped to push through plans for exploring the said land more thoroughly next year with ten or twelve vessels—because in his voyage he had only one ship of fifty 'toneless' and twenty men and food for seven or eight months—and they want to carry out this new project. It is considered certain that the cape of the said land was found and discovered in the past by the men from Bristol who found 'Brasil' as your Lordship well knows. It was called the Island of Brasil, and it is assumed and believed to be the mainland that the men from Bristol found.

"Since your Lordship wants information relating to the first voyage, here is what happened: he went with one ship, his crew confused him, he was short of supplies and ran into bad weather, and he decided to turn back."

Ferdinand of Spain was not pleased with the news and Henry's seeming enthusiasm to pursue his discovery. But he could not afford to interfere or protest too much to the English king because he was trying to woo him into an alliance with Spain against the French, whom Spain wanted out of Italy so she herself could move in and take over the Italian city states. King Henry for his part, also did not want to greatly upset Ferdinand, as he had designs of marrying his son Arthur to Ferdinand's daughter Catherine, and thus by diplomacy and politics gain control of the Spanish throne without having to fight Spain.

While he conducted his diplomacy, Henry VII also went ahead with his plans to follow up Cabot's first voyage. In December 1497 and through January 1498, he had several meetings with the Venetian to discuss his proposals. First, however, there was a matter of pay for Cabot. In January, 1498, he granted the exploder a £20 pension for his work. This may sound like a meagre sum, but this was at a time when ship's captains earned about £8½ a year, provided they were

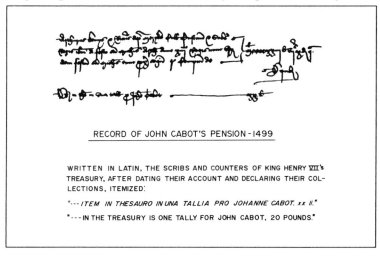

RECORD OF JOHN CABOT'S PENSION-1499

WRITTEN IN LATIN, THE SCRIBS AND COUNTERS OF KING HENRY VII's TREASURY, AFTER DATING THEIR ACCOUNT AND DECLARING THEIR COLLECTIONS, ITEMIZED:

"--- ITEM IN THESAURO IN UNA TALLIA PRO JOHANNE CABOT. xx II."

"--- IN THE TREASURY IS ONE TALLY FOR JOHN CABOT. 20 POUNDS."

employed for fifty weeks of the year! What captain of the time would not be happy about getting a pension that was 120% higher than his annual income? Cabot's pension was to be paid out of the Bristol customs, by which means King Henry ensured that his own treasury funds would not be affected. The Bristol customs coffers were a little tight at the time and Cabot did not see any of his money until two months later.

During his sessions with the King, Cabot learned that Henry had already altered his initial enthusiastic response to Cabot's proposed second voyage. Henry said that he would now send only five ships, instead of ten, and would supply one ship himself if Cabot could find four more. All expenses, however, the parsimonious sovereign declared, would be covered by the merchant backers of the venture. The King's one-fifth share of the profits would, of course, remain the same.

Still, everyone remained agreeable, even though their ambitious plans had to be toned down. Cabot was still determined to win the race to Cathay and Cipango and open up the spice routes to Europe through England. The Bristol merchant princes were anxious to begin exploiting the cod rich waters around the "new-found-land" and start funnelling all the profits from the "stockfish" trade into their own pockets. King Henry had visions of becoming not only one of the most powerful sovereigns in the world, but also the richest.

Cabot and his Bristol benefactors laid out their plan for King Henry. They proposed to sail as far westward as possible until they reached "Cathay" and "Cipango," following the coastline west and south from the "new-found-land" he had discovered the previous year. It seems clear that he intended to sail into the tropics and past the Caribbean lands discovered by Columbus and thus not upset the Spanish by having them think he was infringing on their claims. Cabot, unlike Columbus, correctly believed that Cuba was an island rather than part of the mainland of Asia. He would simply sail on, following the mainland coastline until he reached the Orient. What neither of the explorers could know was that they had discovered a completely "new" world, and that the western hemisphere was a solid land mass with no way through it, except for the difficult Northwest Passage at the top of the world, and the treacherous Drake Passage at the bottom.

What the expedition planned concerning "...all the malefactors...that will go to that country and form a colony..." is not as clear. It is believed that Cabot and his backers may have intended to set up a kind of half-way trading colony, perhaps even in Newfoundland, as he believed he did not have much further to go beyond it to reach the Orient. The half-way post could be used to "storehouse" goods to and from England; spices and jewels coming up by the "coasters" from "Cathay" and "Cipango," and woolens and "stockfish" coming across the Atlantic from England. Its location in the rich fishing grounds of the "new-found-land" would ensure a supply of cod, as well as food for the crews of the ships that ferried the trade goods back and forth between the two destinations.

Early in the New Year of 1498 preparations for the expedition began.

Profile: Henry VII: Machiavellian Monarch

KING HENRY VII OF ENGLAND was born Henry Tudor in Wales in 1457. At a young age he was taken to France where he was raised by his French royal cousins the Valois. As he was distantly related to the Lancastrian line, he decided to enter the War of the Roses that was ongoing in England and depose King Richard III, of the House of York.

He did just that in 1485 when he invaded England with French mercenaries and defeated and killed his cousin King Richard III at the Battle of Bosworth Field. In those days, kings wore their crowns into battle, and when Richard was killed—charging headlong with battle-axe into Henry's personal bodyguard almost reaching the Tudor before he was himself cut down—his crown fell into a hawthorn bush. One of Henry's men found the crown and placed it upon Henry's head. Thus the new King of England was crowned. He ascended the throne on the spot and challenged anyone to try to take his new crown.

Henry had a legitimate, although very slim, claim to the throne, running back to Edward III, but it had been denied to any of his heirs because Edward's eldest son had been born out of wedlock. There were at least a half-dozen others who felt they had a more "legitimate" claim to the throne than the

King Henry VII of England

Tudor "bastards." One of them was Richard III's niece Elizabeth, who Henry promptly married and so settled that claim. Another who had a legal claim was Edward Plantagenet, but the feisty Tudor had him promptly imprisoned and eventually executed. Any other claimants decided it would be too risky to contest the bloody-handed monarch.

Presuming he had put all of the "Pretenders" out of his way, Henry went about the business of building his country. England was by this time considered the "poor cousin" of Europe, and was financially drained by its recently concluded Hundred Years' War with France, and the chaos of its own civil wars, such as the one that Henry had recently concluded by crowning himself king.

Henry vigorously set about the business at hand; making England strong, united, and rich—something he also intended to make himself. He was known as a "penny-pinching, pound-pinching" sovereign, but also noted for his sound and successful business sense. His first order of business after establishing his iron-fisted rule was the finances of the realm.

His domestic rule was remarkable for its tough financial policies, its efficient administration and phenomenal prosperity. England was heavily in debt when Henry took over the reins of power, but his tight-fisted policies soon took it out of the red and into the black. In a few years he had doubled the Crown's revenues, and tripled his own.

He was also able to make his royal coffers bulge by craftily staying out of the wars with other nations. The machinations of his diplomacy, intrigue, and financial wizardry seem to be unsurpassed in the history of the British monarchy. When it looked at one point as though he would have to go to war with France, he was granted money by Parliament to do so but ended up not having to, and somehow blackmailed the King of France into paying him not to go to war! Henry periodically had trouble with the Scots on his borders, and when given the money to go repel them, he would quell the disturbances with half the money allocated and put the other half in his own purse.

The Welsh born king also encouraged trade and commerce as a way of building up his kingdom. He was eager for the schemes of the Bristol and London merchants who proposed opening the avenues of the rich spice trade from

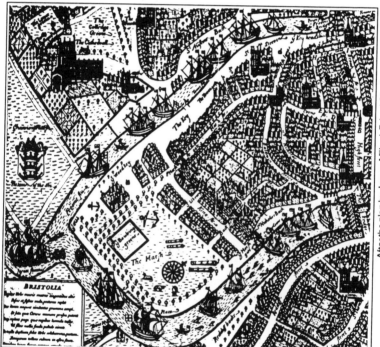

After the plan by James Millerd: Bristol City Archives, England.

Town of Bristol: Detail of a plan of the town about 1670 shows the "Marsh," the commercial part of the town at the junction of the Avon and Frome rivers. The Custom House was here as well as the homes of the major merchants of the port.

"Cathay" and "Cipango" to England, and so enthusiastically sponsored the "voyage of discovery" by John Cabot in 1497 and 1498.

But Henry was also an impatient man. When these excursions failed to produce the profits he expected, he quickly turned his attention to more pragmatic and profitable ventures. He would have his "pound of profit" and was determined that what was "due to Henry" would be "rendered unto Henry." He was the quintessential tax collector: nobody made a crown unless he received part of it. He believed in strict collections, strict courts, and strict punishments. On one occasion an English Earl, who had lavishly entertained the King, was fined £10,000 for "doing the thing too splendidly."

Yet for all his diplomacy abroad, Henry continued to have troubles at home. Although he had an uneasy alliance with the House of York, by virtue of his marriage to Elizabeth, he continued to face Yorkist plots to overthrow him. In 1497 his claim to the throne was challenged by his latest—and bravest—"Pretender." That year, one Perkin Warbeck, Flemish by birth, claimed he was the Duke of York, brother of Edward V, who was supposed murdered with Edward by Richard III in 1483. Warbeck landed in Cornwall in 1497 with 6,000 troops in support of a tax revolt being staged by the Cornishmen. Henry quickly took to the field, rallied his own troops and soon defeated the man who would be king. Warbeck was captured, forced to confess that he was an imposter, and hanged two years later.

Following his victory over this latest "Pretender," Henry once again turned his attention to foreign affairs. His troublesome French "cousins" had been quieted for awhile but his Spanish "cousins" were sabre-rattling, particularly about the Tudor king's latest "trading" expeditions to the "new world." Henry had his own agenda, however—he planned to make an ally of Spain by marrying his eldest son Arthur to the eldest daughter of Spain's King Ferdinand. He was making good progress with his plan when Arthur— named for the legendary King Arthur from whom Henry claimed to be descended—died at age fifteen.

Henry and his "reluctant" wife, Elizabeth, had four children, but she never seemed to recover from the death of her eldest son. In trying to bear another child she died in childbirth. Henry, although he had married both out of connivance and convenience, seemed to truly mourn his loss. But his longterm plans to establish a Tudor dynasty dictated that sentiment be secondary to pragmatism. He had planned to use his son to further his ambitious ends, and in their turn his other children also. Since it would be some time until he could "use" them, he decided to use himself instead.

His target was Joanna of Castille, Spain, the richest heiress in all Europe, but as it turned out she was also the most insane heiress in all Europe. It was said of her that "insanity did not run in her family—it galloped!" Henry, however, persisted in his efforts, proclaiming that all the poor, grief-stricken widow needed was a man who would be a kindly husband to make her well again. But even he relented when he learned that "Crazy Jane"—as she was dubbed in her time—would not go anywhere without the embalmed body of her husband which she carried everywhere with her.

Henry VII died in 1509, still a widower, still parsimonious, still iron-fisted, and still dreaming of making

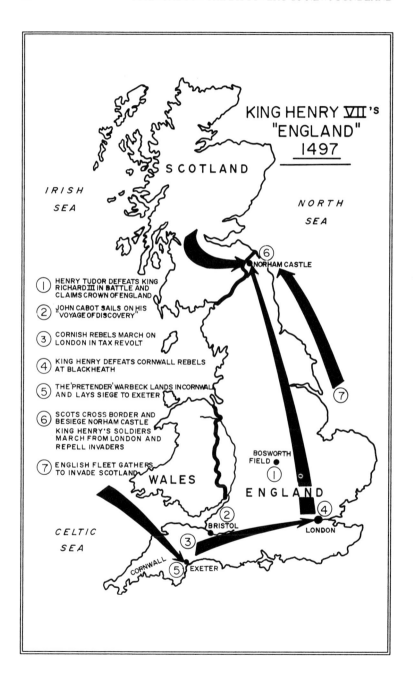

KING HENRY VII'S
"ENGLAND"
1497

SCOTLAND

IRISH
SEA

NORTH
SEA

① NORHAM CASTLE

① HENRY TUDOR DEFEATS KING
RICHARD III IN BATTLE AND
CLAIMS CROWN OF ENGLAND

② JOHN CABOT SAILS ON HIS
"VOYAGE OF DISCOVERY"

③ CORNISH REBELS MARCH ON
LONDON IN TAX REVOLT

④ KING HENRY DEFEATS CORNWALL REBELS
AT BLACKHEATH

⑤ THE 'PRETENDER' WARBECK LANDS IN CORNWALL
AND LAYS SIEGE TO EXETER

⑥ SCOTS CROSS BORDER AND
BESIEGE NORHAM CASTLE
KING HENRY'S SOLDIERS
MARCH FROM LONDON AND
REPELL INVADERS

⑦ ENGLISH FLEET GATHERS
TO INVADE SCOTLAND

⑦

BOSWORTH
FIELD ●

①

WALES

ENGLAND

②
BRISTOL

③

④

LONDON

CELTIC
SEA

CORNWALL

⑤ EXETER

England the richest and most prominent power in Europe. His ends were apparent, and although his means may be questionable, he was in all likelihood, in the words of one observer, "England's first modern King."

Five

"Cabot's Landfall"

JUST WHERE JOHN CABOT LANDED on his voyage of 1497 has been debated and discussed, articulated and argued for over one hundred years. It has been postulated that Cabot landed anywhere between Cape Porcupine, Labrador and Florida— including the island of Newfoundland, Cape Breton, Nova Scotia, Maine or other New England states.

All theories are shored up with evidence, some more flimsy and fanciful than others, yet all have at least a thread of plausibility. Perhaps the least explored "theory" is that given by John Cabot himself. Although he left no log of his voyage, and no journal or diary of the incident appears to exist, the explorer did tell others of his expedition and gave explicit details of it. According to Cabot's own account, he sailed due west from Ireland at approximately 51° 37' North latitude and struck Newfoundland. From the evidence, no other scenario could be more logical.

Much of the speculation concerning Cabot's landfall arises from the confusing documentation of the adventure by his son Sebastian. For centuries, Sebastian Cabot's accounts and claims were believed by most, if not all, chroniclers and investigators as being accurate and legitimate. In the 1850s questions began to arise about the veracity of much Sebastian had recounted to historians of the period.

Although the "mappemonde" and globe which Cabot is known to have produced following his voyages of 1497 and 1498 have not been traced, the information he imparted to many after his returns states clearly where he sailed from, the course he took, the landmass he found, his coastal exploration, and the route of his return voyages. John Cabot was a skilled mariner who could not have deviated from his set course by some 400-500 miles without knowing it and making attempts to correct it. John Cabot's own assertion that he had found a "new isle," tells us that he knew he had discovered an island and not the mainland he had been seeking. The claims that he had landed in Labrador or Maine, or some other New England state can therefore be eliminated. But the claim that he landed on Cape Breton Island in Nova Scotia has had much support in recent times and begs some scrutiny.

Again, the reason for the controversy over whether John Cabot's landfall was in Newfoundland or Cape Breton is due to his "unfilial" son Sebastian, who in later years claimed that it was he, not his father, who had actually made the "discovery" of 1497 and that he had captained the second voyage to the "new isle" in 1498. In 1544, Sebastian, working for Spain as that country's "Pilot Major," or Chief of Navigation, himself had a "mappenmonde," or map of the world, made, on which he had his own information portrayed. On it, Sebastian placed the landfall of his father at Cape North on Cape Breton Island.

Sebastian's reasons for this piece of duplicity were not questioned or understood for almost four hundred years.

Photo: B. Fardy (1993)

Memorial at Cape Bonavista to John Cabot gives a brief account of the explorer's supposed landfall at the site in English and French (at left), and Italian (at right). Although it does not claim "unequivocal identification" of the site, it "allows" that "local tradition" claims it to be Cabot's landfall in Newfoundland

Under studious scrutiny it was found that many of the place names on his map were French in origin. As one investigator commented; "...a thorough perusal of this document discloses some very singular things. For instance, we can see the nomenclature of some places given by Jacques Cartier in 1534 and 1535. How can these French names be explained on the Cabotian map? where did Cabot get them?"

If Sebastian had, as he claimed, landed at Cape Breton in 1496, why did he use French names known to be derived from Cartier's explorations to name landmarks and sites that he himself (or at least his father) would have named in English, or Italian, if they had actually been there almost forty years before Cartier?

It has been suggested that Sebastian Cabot "engineered" his map to gain favour with the English, by whom he was desperately trying to be repatriated. He likely believed that if he could establish a previous claim for England as having landed on the mainland of the "new world" which she had "discovered," the English could contest the French claims to Acadia and "New France," which they were attempting to establish following the voyage of Cartier. The English were now seriously thinking about establishing a "New England" in the "new world," and a claim to it prior to Cartier's voyages would stand it in good stead when contesting the claims of the French.

Other evidence of the "misinformation" give by Sebastian Cabot on his 1544 "mappenmonde" is contained in the legend, which is information Sebastian supplied himself. An entry in the legend uses words which assert that "...I suppose that it was...," and "...I think it was because...," and "...he called...," and "...they had...,"—words not likely to be used by someone who had done a deed himself to describe and recount it.

Henry Harrisse, a noted historian of the late nineteenth century, and considered an authority on the Cabot voyages in his time, was the first to analyze the evidence of John Cabot's son. Of Sebastian Cabot he concluded, his "...statements as regards the first landfall on the continent of North America are in absolute contradiction to the legends and delineations of the planisphere of 1544, and that these in their turn, are based entirely on the discoveries made by Jacques Cartier in 1534 and 1536 and not at all on Cabot's."

If Sebastian Cabot's claim that Cape Breton was the landfall of his father's voyage in 1497 was made to convince the English that they had a rightful and historic claim to the "mainland" of North America, and not just an island, then he had defeated his very purpose. Had he, or even his father actually landed at Cape Breton, then they would have known that it, like Newfoundland, was also an island!

Claims that Cabot's landfall was made at Cape North on Cape Breton Island emerged only about sixty years ago—some say only because of an effort to increase tourism. When a monument to Cabot was erected in Montreal in 1935, the claim was made that Cabot had landed on Cape Breton Island—if not, as some would have liked to claim, in Montreal itself. The monument was erected and dedicated, but not with the originally intended dedication. The words prepared for the plaque had to be changed due to the protests of historians who did not agree that Cape Breton was the landfall of Cabot.

On May 25th, 1935, Commander Catelli of the Italian Consulate in Montreal, wrote the Governor of New-foundland as follows: "On the occasion of the unveiling of this monument in honour of John Cabot, offered the City of Montreal by the Italian Canadian Colony, we wish to associate Newfoundland in our celebration as the first land sighted and discovered by this great Navigator." The Governor of Newfoundland replied with a polite, "thank-you very much."

Although Montreal refused to officially recognize Cape Breton as Cabot's landfall, Cape Breton was not so willing to follow suit. That same year, the island celebrated the 150th anniversary of the founding of the city of Sydney, and proclaimed that their island was the site of Cabot's landfall. When the Newfoundland press protested their claim and asked for proof, none was forthcoming.

Air Photo of Cape Bonavista: showing Green Ridge, elevation 350 feet. It would have been the most visible point of land to Cabot had he been blown or carried southwestward from his course by the strong Labrador current.

Regardless of the political and historical debates Sebastian Cabot's claims would cause in later centuries, the reasons for his connivance were deeply steeped in the political intrigues of his own time. In his prestigious position in Spain he could not have failed to know that both the Spanish and Portuguese had recognized John Cabot's voyages. By 1502, after the voyages of Corte-Real, both these kingdoms

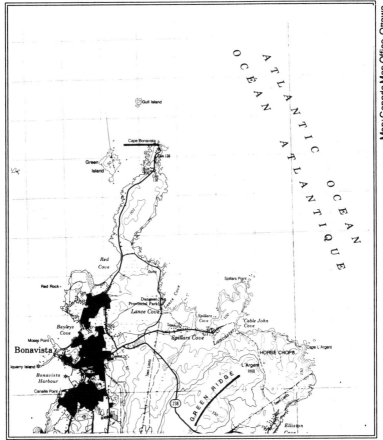

Current topagraphical map showing Capr Bonavista and Green Ridge; elevation 350 feet.

had drawn up maps which acknowledged the Venetian's explorations. In Portugal the "Cantino Map," and in Spain, the "La Cosa Map," identified "Cavo de Ynglaterre"— "English Cape"—and "Mars descubierta por Inglesses"—Sea discovered by the English."

Concrete evidence that Cabot landed somewhere on the island of Newfoundland comes from an unbiased source only three years after Cabot's expeditions. Returning from a voyage of exploration to Newfoundland in 1500, Gasper Corte-Real brought back to Portugal fifty-seven of the "natives" of the island and pieces of "a broken sword, inlaid with gold, which we are convinced was made in Italy, and one of the children had in his ears two pieces of silver which most certainly seem to have been made in Venice...." Since neither the Spanish nor the Portuguese had explored this part of the Atlantic at all, the only possible explanation for these "artifacts" is that one of Cabot's crews, if not Cabot himself, had left them in Newfoundland.

Just where on the island of Newfoundland Cabot made his historic landfall has been debated and discussed almost as hotly as the argument about whether it was Newfoundland or some other place. Traditionally, it has been held that Cape Bonavista was the landfall, but further inves-

Photo: B. Fardy (1993)

The rugged, deep georges and high, steep cliffs of Cape Bonavista on both its east coast (left) and west coast (right), makes landing there extremely difficult.

tigation and study holds up good evidence that the explorer's landfall may have been further north on the Great Northern Peninsula.

The accepted contention among many observers is that Cape Bonavista must have been Cabot's landfall because his course was drastically altered by the Labrador Current and drift ice from the north. There is every possibility that Cabot did encounter ice on his voyage, but there is nothing that tells he definitely did. His own account says nothing about ice.

By late June or early July, ice conditions off Newfoundland's east coast are usually not severe enough to impede shipping. By then the ice has usually moved well off to the southeast of the island, leaving the northeast coast approachable. The drift of the Labrador Current is not so strong as to alter the course of a vessel if its navigator is skilled and diligent, although Cabot's small wooden ship was, of course, not a modern ice-breaker. While it is possible that Cabot encountered ice and fog, he was not sailing by dead reckoning only. He was supplied with the latest navigational instruments which he apparently knew how to use with precision.

Cabot's own report of his voyage of 1497 states that he left Bristol and sailed northwards to Ireland, where he departed from Dursey Head. For the Bristol men who regularly sailed to Iceland and westward in search of the "isle of Brasil" or other fabled lands of St. Brendan and the Vikings, this was a favoured point of departure westward. Geographically, it is the most westerly point of Ireland and sailors who spied that point wasted little time in getting "sea room," as the area was known for its treacherous waters.

Air Photo of Quirpon Island: showing Cape Dégrat off the northern tip of Newfoundland. At an elevation of 500 feet, it was the most visible landmark for more than fifty miles for Cabot who was sailing westward at approximately 50° latitude.

It was Cabot's intention to sail a high, short latitude course on a due west "easting." He believed the distance in northern latitude would be shorter than any in an equatorial region. The Venetian mariner set his course at 51° 33' North latitude from Dursey Head and used his skills and instruments to keep him on that course.

Cabot likely encountered the Greenland current which, although weak, probably carried him a little northward from his course. Later, he would have been carried a little southward by the stronger Labrador Current, but Cabot did not have to be concerned about being "blown off" course; with his sophisticated navigational equipment he could quickly find it again.

It appears the only real obstacle Cabot encountered was the storm "about two or three days out" before his landfall. This and the variation he detected in his compass probably altered his course, but being diligent, the Venetian corrected for the variance and probably did not drift too far off his "true" westerly course. Sometime during the night of June 23rd, he probably sensed the "loom of the Land," picking up the smells of the fir and spruce forests, noticing the low lying clouds and seeing and hearing the calls of the sea birds. As dawn broke he saw the rugged, 500 foot high, barren landmass of Cape Dégrat rising out of the sea a little to his starboard side and fixed his course towards it.

Steering southwest of his course, he probably passed the large Belle Isle, which he named "St. John's Island," after the feast day of that saint, and sailed on for the more extensive landmass of the great northern peninsula which told him it was the "mainland" he was seeking. Belle Isle rises 500 feet out of the sea, but Cabot would have recognized that it was merely an island, and headed for Quirpon Island with its 500 feet high Cape Dégrat, since it appeared to be a part of the northern peninsula and therefore the mainland. At fifteen or twenty miles distance from the island of Newfoundland, he

Current Topographical map of Quirpon Island showing Cape Dégrat at elevation 502 feet and at 50° 19' west latitude.

would not have seen the landmass of Labrador which would be a further twenty miles or so from Belle Isle and the great northern peninsula.

Once having sighted Cape Dégrat and heading towards it, Cabot soon saw that the rocky, barren island of Quirpon offered no place to land. He set his sails south along the coast of the great northern peninsula and about five miles south came to the forested, sheltered harbour at Griquet. From there he took his bearings.

He found that he was at 50°33' North latitude, very close to the latitude of Dursey Head, Ireland. He had sighted Cape Dégrat at 50°37' North latitude just slightly in a northwesterly direction. Cabot's *Mathew* had landed only about five miles from where Leif Erickson had landed at L'Anse aux Meadows.

As Admiral S.E. Morison observed, "...what an extraordinary coincidence? The first two Europeans to discover North America, half a millennium apart, hit that vast continent within a few miles of each other...." Considering that Cape Dégrat is at 50°37' North latitude, and Griquet Harbour at 50°33' North latitude—exactly the same latitude as Dursey Head, Ireland,—this must be, again in the words of Admiral Morison, "one of the most accurate and successful bits of celestial navigation in the early era of discovery."

After almost a month of "coasting," Cabot returned to his "landfall," set his course on the same latitude he had calculated he had arrived in the "new-found-land," and set his sails for home.

Photo: B. Fardy (1993)

John Cabot: The statue of the explorer looks down from the heights of Cape Bonavista upon the "new-founde-land" he discovered in 1497.

Profile: Sebastian Cabot: Explorer or Pretender

SEBASTIAN CABOT, son of the famous John Cabot, has been written about and debated about for over 400 years by scholars and historians. He has been branded as the "unfilial son," who was "imp-tongued...boastful...vain," a "dishonest man" who was an "unmitigated liar" whose word "no reliance can be placed upon," and as the "usurper of his father's claim." He was seen to be a man of "constant mendacity and treason," a man who was "a great schemer," and who even went so far as to claim he had "a divine revelation" on his deathbed.

John Cabot's son, Sebastian, was born about 1484 in Venice where his family was then living. He was later taken to Spain and then England where his father was engaged by Bristol merchants to undertake the historic voyage to the new

Sebastian Cabot

world. After his father's presumed death in 1498, young Sebastian was apprenticed to Bristol merchants where he learned the skills of cartography and navigation.

We can only speculate about what young Sebastian learned from his explorer father, but although he likely did not accompany his father on the historic voyage to Newfoundland, he may have been privy to information that his father wanted kept secret.

In 1508, whether because of his father's reputation or his own competence, he was granted permission by the King of England to take an expedition to the northwest in the wake of his father. Henry VII was impressed by the work of the young son of his previous captain of exploration and allowed him to outfit two ships at his own expense to pursue the adventure his father had begun.

Sebastian sailed northwest into what would later be named Hudson Strait, and may even have reached Hudson's Bay. He found the route difficult, as one historian of the period put it, "even in the month of July he found great icebergs floating in the sea and almost continuous daylight." When he attempted to press on, Cabot's crew mutinied and forced him to retreat to more hospitable seas. Sebastian Cabot was probably the first explorer since the Vikings to sail into Hudson's Strait, but he was not the last, nor was he the last to have a mutinous crew. The man for whom the strait was named came over a hundred years after him, but Henry Hudson was not as fortunate as Cabot. Cabot survived his mutiny; Hudson was murdered by his crew.

After the mutiny, Cabot coasted south along the east coast of North America perhaps as far south as Florida before returning to England. Arriving there he found that King Henry VII was dead and the country was preoccupied with the coronation ceremonies of seventeen year old Henry VIII. His unsuccessful expedition attracted little or no attention, but its results were to linger for over one hundred years.

The new King was more interested in domestic comforts than foreign exploits and Sebastian Cabot appears to have been enlisted by the British Army. In 1512 he was posted to

Spain with the forces of the Marquis of Dorset who, with the Spanish, were preparing to invade France. For the next thirty-five years, Cabot would serve the Spanish Crown.

About 1515 he married a Spanish woman named Catalina Medrano and they had one daughter, Elizabeth, who was his only heir. During his early years in Spain, Sebastian was employed as a pilot of the Casa de Contraction where he reviewed maps and charts, especially those of the "new-found-land," which he was believed to have exclusive knowledge of. In 1518 he was promoted to the job of Major Pilot, and as head of the navigation school was responsible for the updating of the West Indies map, the Padron Real.

In 1521 and again in 1524, Sebastian was involved in attempts to interest King Henry VIII and the Bristol merchants in his further plans to find a "northwest passage." Both his attempts failed, due largely to the intervention of the Drapers Company who were skeptical of Cabot's abilities as a mariner.

Spain, however, had no reservations about his competence. In 1526, Cabot was sent on a four year expedition to South America where he explored the Plate River of Paraguay, looking for the southwest passage to Cathay. His instructions to his ship's captains on this voyage shows the usual paradox of contemporary thinking. There was "to be no dicing, carding, tabling; morning and evening prayers are to be said...." He also ordered that, "the natives of strange countries are to be enticed on board and made drunk with your beer and wine, for then you shall know the secrets of their hearts." He also warned his men to be "cautious about certain creatures with men's heads and the tails of fishes, who swim with bows and arrows, about the fords and bays, and live on human flesh." This is no doubt a reference to the South American Indians, some tribes of which were head hunters and believed to practise cannibalism.

When he left Spain for South America, Cabot had charge of four ships and 200 men, but when he returned in 1530 he had only one ship and twenty-four men. He was tried on criminal charges and found guilty, but two years later he was again working as Spain's Pilot-Major.

For the next sixteen years Cabot continued in the employ of the Spanish Crown but he also pursued his dream of finding a "northwest passage" for England. During these years he negotiated with Venetian merchants and England about his proposed venture. In 1546 the English Privy Council sent him money to buy his passage back to England.

Once there he espoused his theory of finding a shorter route to the Orient via a "northwest passage." He was listened to but no action was taken on his proposals. Spain, having learned of his scheming, demanded that he be returned to Spanish service. Henry VIII refused, saying that Cabot was a British subject and if he did not wish to return to Spain then he could not be forced.

During the last ten years of his life, Sebastian Cabot seemed to be a changed man. He was observed as being a most amiable man, well-liked, trusted, and even fun-loving. Shortly before his death in 1577, one English sea captain said of him; "the good old gentleman...who went down to Gravesend to wish God-speed to an exploring expedition, made great cheer at the Inn for the ship's company and entered into the dance himself amongst the rest of the young and lusty company."

History has not treated Sebastian Cabot with much favour, yet he was an accomplished explorer and geographer. Given the political intrigues of his time and his personal aspirations, perhaps the worst and best that should be said of him is that although he was a conniver, he was also a survivor.

Six

"Cabot's Second Voyage"

O~N~ F~EBRUARY~ 3rd, 1498, John Cabot received his second "letters patent" for his second voyage in the employ of King Henry VII of England. The petition to the King and his reply reads:

> "To the kinge: Pleas it your highnesse, of your moste noble and habundaunt grace, to graunte to John Kabotto, Venician, your gracious letters patentes...and he shal contynullay praye to God for the preservacion of your moste noble and roiall astate longe to endure."

> "H(en)R(icus) Rex: To all men to whom thies presentis shall come, send gretyng: Knowe ye that we of our grace especiall and for dyvers causis us movyng we have geven and graunten...to our wel beloved John Kabotto, Venician, sufficiente auctorite and power that he by hym, his deputie or deputies sufficient may take at his pleasure vi englisshe shippes in any porte or portes or other place within this our realm of Englond or obeisaunce...,and theym convey and lede to the londe and Iles of late founde by the seid John in oure name and by our commaundemente, paying for theym and every of theym as and if we shuld in or for our owen cause paye and noon otherwise."

Cabot was authorized to outfit six ships but he could only raise four. Henry, as he had promised, supplied a fifth, possibly one of his own Royal naval vessels. All the ships were armed and provisioned for one year. The expenses were all paid for by the Bristol merchants, and the explorer was authorized to employ any captain or seamen he wanted, provided they wanted to go.

During the recruitment, King Henry invoked an old, seldom used law, which demanded that anyone leaving the realm have a "passport." In this case he deemed it necessary to reinstate that law so as to keep just anyone from sailing to the "new-found-land" and cashing in on the bonanza that was believed to be out there.

The five ships were outfitted during the months of March and April at Bristol. King Henry had sent his ship, a crew and arms, but no cargo. It was left to the Bristol and London merchants, whom the Bristol merchant princes had persuaded to join the venture, to fill the holds of the ships with trade goods. That this was a trading expedition there is no doubt. The merchants filled their ships with bales of their English woolens; hats, caps, socks, and the famous West England blankets and yard cloth. It is not likely they were preparing to trade the expensive world renowned goods for codfish.

By the end of April the tiny fleet was ready to sail. The exact date of departure is not known but is believed to have been in the first week of May. Many prominent Bristol and London merchants were aboard the ships as well as a couple of envoys of foreign governments, who were represented as "poor Italian friars," but in reality turned out to be something quite different. One of them, Giovanni Antonio Carbonariis,

This statue of John Cabot (left) looks down from the heights of Cape Bonavista upon the "new-founde-land" he discovered in 1947. In the view on the right he "appears" to be standing upon the heights of his landfall at Cape Bonavista.

was a mercenary Milanese cleric, known to be a man of some reputation and means. Another was a garrulous Spanish "friar" named Buil, who had accompanied Columbus on his second voyage and was known to have been a constant troublemaker. It seems that Spain and Italy were continuing their intrigue and had their spies planted aboard the expedition to report on it, and possibly even to cause disruptions and trouble.

Shortly after the fleet's departure from Avonsmouth and not far off the coast of Ireland the ships ran into rough weather. One of them was "damaged" and returned to Ireland to be repaired. The other four continued on their journey. One period historian, Polydore Vergil, an Italian priest who lived in England from 1502 for almost fifty years and wrote a history of that country, believed that the vessel that returned to port was Cabot's, and that after repairs he again continued the voyage. Another possibility is that the ship that returned to Ireland was Cabot's, and may not have been damaged, but that the troublesome "friar" Buil had begun his antics and Cabot returned to port to put him ashore and rid of him.

Whatever the reasons for the return to Ireland, what happened next is shrouded in mystery. History records that none of the ships returned home, and that John Cabot and all his crews were lost at sea. Where they travelled and what they encountered may never be known for certain. Perhaps the small fleet ran into a raging storm, encountered heavy ice and were crushed, or were swept ashore on the rocky coast of Newfoundland.

All are very plausible scenarios, but it is unlikely that all the ships would have encountered the same conditions at the same time. We know that at least one of them was trailing behind, possibly even Cabot's ship itself.

The ships were provisioned for a one year voyage, and there is some evidence that at least one of them, if not more, returned from the expedition. While they were at sea however, the political intrigues continued on land. In July, 1498, the Spanish ambassador to England, Pedro de Ayala, wrote his sovereigns about the latest ventures of King Henry:

"I well believe that your Highnesses have heard how the King of England has equipped a fleet to discover certain Islands and mainland that certain persons who set out last year for the same have testified that they have found. I have seen the chart which the discoverer has drawn, who is another Genoese like Columbus, and has been in Seville and Lisbon procuring to find those who would help him in this enterprise....The King determined to despatch an expedition because he had the certainty that they had found land last year. The fleet consists of five ships provisioned for one year....The Genoese went on his course. I have seen the course and distance he takes, think that the land they have found or seek is that which your Highnesses possess, for it is the end of that which belongs to your Highnesses by the convention with Portugal. It is hoped that they will return by September....I believe the distance is not 400 leagues. And I told him that I thought they were the Islands discovered by your Highnesses, and I even gave him a reason but he would not hear it; as I believe your Highnesses now have intelligence of all, as well as the chart or mappe-monde that this Genoese has made, I do not send it now though I have it here; and to me it seems very false, to give out that they are not the said Islands."

What Ayala was attempting to tell Ferdinand and Isabella was that he believed that Henry VII had sent Cabot and his ships on a voyage to Spanish claimed territory. This was not true of course, but it had enough effect to spur the Spanish and Portuguese kings into action. They loudly decried the English King's excursions, and Henry VII, preoccupied as he was with domestic problems and trying to cement foreign alliances, relented a little.

The Iberian kings' protests may account for the lack of knowledge of the second voyage of Cabot. No concrete knowledge of its fate, or results, exist, but much has been speculated. Its dismal failure and the believed loss of its captain, Cabot, may have persuaded Henry to downplay the excursion and hope that its result would not embarrass him, or further incite the Iberian monarchs.

It is possible that one, or even two, of Cabot's ships sailed the North Atlantic coast as far as Florida and returned to Bristol to recount their exploits. Evidence that at least one ship returned after landing in the "new-found-land" is recorded by contemporary historians. The chronicler, Fabian, reported that Cabot, or at least one of the ships in his expedition, brought back with them three natives "which he (Cabot) presented to the King (Henry VII) in the fourteenth year of his reign (1499)."

The account states that, "This year also were brought unto the King, three men taken in the New-found-Island, that before I spoke of in William Purchas' time. These were clothed with beast's skins, and ate raw flesh and spoke a language that no man could understand them, in their demeanour like to brute beasts, whom the King kept a time after, of the which upon two years past after, I saw two apparelled after the manner of Englishmen in Westminster Palace, which at that time I could not discern from Englishmen, till I learned what they were. But as for speech, I heard none of them utter one world."

Exactly who returned with these "natives" is unknown, but Cabot himself was still believed to be alive. His yearly pension of £20 was paid by the royal treasury for the period Michealmass 1498 to Michealmass 1499. The pension was probably paid to his wife who was then living in Bristol on St. Nycoles Street in a house that was being kept rented by Cabot for £2 per year. After 1499 the payment of Cabot's pension stopped. For the public record he had not returned from his voyage of 1498 and was now presumed "lost at sea."

History does not record any further evidence of Cabot, except that one chronicler believes that he survived the voyage and did not return to England, but sailed to Spain or Portugal, where he afterwards participated in joint ventures of the English-Portuguese expeditions to the "new world." But the Portuguese discovery in 1500-1501 of "a piece of a broken gilt sword which seemed to have been made in Italy, and a pair of silver ear-rings which appeared to be of Venetian manufacture," in Newfoundland, could mean that Cabot or one of his ships had landed in the "new-found-land" and engaged in a hostile encounter with the natives. If this occurred, it accounts for what happened to the ship and the crew. If they were attacked and pursued aboard their ship, which could not make sail, the entire crew may have been slaughtered, the ship fired and sank, and no trace of any of the encounter left to history.

Whatever Cabot's fate, he could not have known the significance of his "discovery." He believed, like Columbus, that he could find a route to "Cathay" and "Cipango," but what he did discover was a completely "new world." At first, he was probably frustrated and perhaps even disappointed. If he did survive his 1498 voyage, he probably became even more determined to explore exactly what it was he had "discovered." It turned out to be a continent that would defy passage for more than fifty years, but that eventually produced two great democratic nations renowned for social and economic fairness and justice—the United States of America, and Canada.

Profile: Cabot Commemorated

JOHN CABOT has been called the explorer who made the "intellectual discovery of North America," as opposed to the accidental "discovery" made by the Vikings and perhaps others. As such, he has been honoured and commemorated by many countries and cities; Genoa where he was born, Venice where he grew up, Spain where he lived, and Bristol from where he made his historic voyages. In the new world he is claimed as an "adopted" son by Newfoundland, Nova Scotia, Quebec, and even some Americans in the New England states. In the words of one observer, "great men are often claimed by many communities."

Cabot has been commemorated by having everything from stamps to schools named for him. Quebec, for whatever obscure reason, remembers him with "Cabot Square" and its "quaint" monument in west-end Montreal. In Cape Breton, the scenic "Cabot Trail" through the "highlands" of that island connects it to the mainland of Nova Scotia. Near Cape North on that island in Aspy Bay, Cape Bretoners erected a monument thirty-five years ago for a "Cabot Day Observance" which saw them declare that Cape North was the "official landfall" of Cabot in 1497. Between there and the southwest tip of Newfoundland a ninety mile stretch of the Atlantic Ocean has been named the Cabot Strait.

In Newfoundland, the only correct claimant of Cabot as an "adopted son," the explorer has been honoured for more than a hundred years, commemorated with everything from ships to statues.

In 1897, the Newfoundland government issued two stamps to commemorate the 400th anniversary of Cabot's

STAMPS COMMEMORATE CABOT'S DISCOVERY OF NEWFOUNDLAND

Cabot's ship *Matthew* leaving The Avon. Issued June 24, 1897 to commemorate the 400th anniversary of Cabot's discovery. It is believed this is actually a representation of the Flagship of Columbus, and not the *Mat-*

Stamps: Courtesy of J.V. Fardy

Cabot's ship *Matthew*. Issued April, 1949, to celebrate Newfoundland's entry into confederation.

Cabot – "Him that found the New Isle." Issued in 1897 to commemorate the 400th anniversary of Cabot's discovery. (The portrait is actually one of Sebastian, his son. There is to date no known portrait of John.)

Cabot in the *Matthew* off Cape Bonavista – 1497. Issued June, 1947 to commemorate the 450th anniversary of Cabot's discovery.

discovery of the "new-found-land." Both these stamps were years later found to be in error in their portrayals, owing to the lack of information about the Cabot voyages and the man himself. In 1947 they issued a commemorative celebrating the 450th anniversary of Cabot's discovery of the island. Two years later, the Canadian Government issued a stamp on April 1st, 1949 to celebrate Newfoundland's entry into Confederation.

1897 was a banner year for Cabot commemoration. That year it was decided that the city of St. John's would build a "tower" atop the 600-foot-high Signal Hill overlooking the "narrows," the entrance to St. John's harbour. At the same time, the city of Bristol in England decided it would build a "sister tower" in memory of the man which both cities claimed as their adopted son. Bristol's Cabot Tower was built atop Brandon Hill, overlooking the "Marsh," where Cabot and many of the Bristol merchant princes lived during those historic days. Its erection, however, went much more smoothly than that of the Cabot Tower at St. John's.

The conception of the project was opposed by some who felt it was akin to "placing a silk hat on the head of a man who had not a decent pair of boots to keep his feet warm," implying that the country was too poor to afford such a frivolous project. Others felt that it would be "an imposing edifice to greet the first gaze of a mariner; something worthy of an important seaport like St. John's." Most of the populace simply felt that the money being raised for the construction of the "tower" could be better spent on a fishermen's insurance fund or a public hospital.

But the commemorative committee persevered and on June 22nd, 1897, the cornerstone for the tower was laid atop Signal Hill by dignitaries and throngs of the public who so vigorously had protested its frivolousness that "bunting is at a premium, and even the millinery stores are getting ransacked for fancy fabrics and feathers suitable for decorative purposes."

The laying of the corner stone for "Cabot Tower" atop Signal Hill on June 22, 1897.

The "Tower" was completed in 1900, and a year later was the site of the reception of the first wireless signal across the Atlantic Ocean received by Marconi. Ironically, Marconi, another Italian like John Cabot before him, was foiled in his attempts to establish the first trans-Atlantic wireless station in the world. The Anglo-American Company, which controlled the Atlantic Cable and the telegraph system in Newfoundland, blocked Marconi's effort, and he left for Nova Scotia where his ideas were more welcome.

Cabot Tower continued as an important communications station for several years, broadcasting weather and ice conditions to fishing stations in Labrador and isolated communities throughout the island until as late as 1960. Later it became a part of the Signal Hill national historic park, where today it houses a museum showcasing the history of the

Marconi's assistants prepare to receive the first trans-Atlantic message on Signal Hill.

tower and that of the 600-foot-high hill which has played such a prominent role in the history of St. John's.

The province of Newfoundland has further remembered Cabot by naming the highway which winds from the Trans-Canada up the Bonavista peninsula to the town of the same name, the Cabot Highway. A statue and plaque in his memory have also been erected near the town.

In St. John's, several businesses carry his name and a street in the old downtown core of the city bears his name. A statue of Cabot stands sentinel in front of the government offices at Confederation Building. A scientific research vessel of the Canadian Coast Guard is also named for him, and in recent years the Newfoundland-Labrador College of Trades and Technology has been renamed the Cabot Institute of Technology.

Photo: B. Fardy, 1993

Cabot Tower stands sentinel atop the summit of Signal Hill, on the north side of the "Narrows," the entrance to St. John's harbour, and gateway to the historic city

Bibliography

Ceram, C.W.; *The First American.* Harcourt, Brace, Jovonovich, Inc., New York: 1971.

Cumming, W.P.; and R.A. Skelton and D.B. Quinn: *The Discovery of North America.* McClelland and Stewart, Toronto and Montreal: 1972.

Dor-Ner, Zvi; and William G. Scheller: *Columbus: The Age of Discovery.* William Morrow and Co., New York: 1991.

Fardy, B.D.: "Canada's First White Settlers." *Canadian Frontier.* Amtonsen Publishing Ltd., New Westminster, B.C.: 1978.

Froncek, Thomas: *The Norsemen.* Time-Life Books, New York: 1974.

Harrington, Michael: "Spanish Province of Terra Nova." *Evening Telegram;* St. John's, Oct. 24, 1977.

Herm, Gerhard: *The Celts: The People Who Came Out of the Darkness.* St. Martin's Press, New York: 1977.

Howley, James P.: *The Beothucks or Red Indians: The Aboriginal Inhabitants of Newfoundland.* Cambridge University Press, Cambridge: 1915.

Humble, Richard: *The Explorers.* Time-Life Books, Alexandria, Virginia: 1978.

Ingstad, Helge: Trans. by Erin J. Friis. *Westward To Vinland.* Harper Colophon Books - Harper and Rowe, New York: 1972.

Jackman, L.J.: "Cabot." *Newfoundland Quarterly,* Vol. 60, No. 1, St. John's: 1961.

Jackman, L.J.: "Criticism of Cabot Puts Cart Before Horse." *Newfoundland Quarterly,* Vol. 58, No. 3, St. John's: 1959.

Jackman, L.J.: "New Light on Cabot Discovery." *Newfoundland Quarterly,* Vol. 58, No. 1, St. John's: 1959.

Jelks, Edward B.: *Archaeological Exploration at Signal Hill, Newfoundland.* National Historic Sites Service, Parks Canada, Ottawa: 1973.

Jones, Gwyn: *A History of the Vikings.* Oxford University Press, Oxford and New York: 1984.

Lamontagne, Yves: "History Gives Gasper Corte Real Credit for Cabot's Discovery of Newfoundland." *Newfoundland Quarterly,* Vol. 58, No. 3, St. John's: 1959

Lehane, Brendan: *The Northwest Passage.* Time-Life Books; Alexandria, Virginia: 1981.

Maddocks, Melvin: *The Atlantic Crossing*. Time-Life Books; Alexandria, Virginia: 1981.

Magnusson, Magnus; and Hermann Palsson, eds.: *The Vinland Sagas: The Norse Discovery of America*. Penguin Books; Middlesex, England: 1975.

Morison*, Samuel Eliot: *The Great Explorers*. Oxford University Press; New York: 1978.

(*note Morison is spelled Morrison throughout the copy)

Morris, Sir Edward: "Bristol and St. John's - A Tale of Two Cities," *Newfoundland Quarterly*, Vol. 10, No. 4, St. John's: 1911.

Mowat, Farley: *West Viking*. McClelland and Stewart Ltd., Toronto: 1973.

Munn, W.A.: "John Cabot's Landfall." *Newfoundland Quarterly*. Vol. 36, No. 1; St. John's: 1936.

Mustard, Cam; and Amy Zeiler: *Signal Hill: An Illustrated History*. Nfld. Historic Trust Assoc., St. John's: 1982.

Neary, Peter; and Patrick O'Flaherty, eds.: "Johan* Day's Letter (1497)." *By Great Waters: A Newfoundland and Labrador Anthology*. University of Toronto Press; Toronto: 1974

(*note spelled John elsewhere in text).

Norton-Taylor, Duncan: *The Celts*. Time-Life Books, New York: 1974.

O'Dea, Fabian: "Cabot's Landfall - Yet Again." *Newfoundland Quarterly*. Vol. 6, No. 2; St. John's: 1971.

O'Dea, Fabian: "Early Maps of Newfoundland." *The Book of Newfoundland*, Vol. III. Newfoundland Book Publishers Ltd., St. John's: 1967.

O'Neill, Paul: *The Oldest City: The Story of St. John's, Newfoundland*. Press Porcepic, Erin, Ontario: 1975.

Parsons, John: "John Cabot." *The Canadian Encyclopedia*. Hurtig Publishing Ltd., Edmonton: 1988.

Pierson, Dr. Frank W.: "Cabotian Literature." *Newfoundland Quarterly*, Vol. 34, No. 4, St. John's: 1935.

Prowse, D.W.: *A History of Newfoundland*. McMillan and Co., London and New York: 1895.

Rowe, Frederick W.: *A History of Newfoundland and Labrador*. McGraw-Hill, Ryerson Ltd., Toronto, Montreal, New York: 1980.

Saunders, Robert: "Cabot's Landfall in the New World," *Newfoundland Quarterly*, Vol. 59, No. 4, St. John's: 1960.

Saunders, Robert: "Stand Fast For Bonavista," *Newfoundland Quarterly*, Vol. 56, No. 1; St. John's: 1957.

Selwyn-Brown, Dr. Arthur: "Newfoundland A Basque Colony," *Newfoundland Quarterly*, Vol. 32, No. 2; St. John's: 1932.

Selwyn-Brown, Dr. Arthur: "Ships of Early Atlantic Voyages," *Newfoundland Quarterly*, Vol. 21, No. 2; St. John's: 1921.

Smallwood, Joseph R.; editor: *The Book of Newfoundland, Vols. I - VI*. Newfoundland Book Publishers (1967) Ltd.; St. John's: 1975.

Smallwood, Joseph R.: *Encyclopedia of Newfoundland, Vols. I - III*. Newfoundland Book Publishers Ltd., St. John's: 1981-1991.

Wernick, Robert: *The Vikings*. Time-Life Books, Alexandria, Virginia: 1979.

White, Jack: "Viking Tales and a Street in St. John's," *Evening Telegram*, St. John's: Feb. 29, 1992.

Whiteley, George C.: "Was Cape Dégrat Cabot's Landfall?", *Evening Telegram*; St. John's: June 23, 1984.

Williamson, James A.: *The Cabot Voyages and Bristol Discovery Under Henry VII*. The Hakluyt Society, Cambridge, England: 1962.